Nature's Flying Jewels –

A Semi-Organized Compilation of Hummingbird Information, Data, and Trivia

A collaborative effort by

Bill and Terrie Merritt

Ozarklake Distinct Decor
Camdenton, MO 65020
573-286-0491
info@ozarklake.net
www.ozarklake.net

FOREWORD

Once upon a time there was a lady who collected everything hummingbird. She accumulated little glass hummingbirds, calendars featuring hummer pictures, hummingbird waterglobes and music boxes, hummingbird art and wall hangings, hummingbird magnets, hummingbird candles and candleholders - every little (and big) knick-knack you can imagine. She was fascinated by the feisty little iridescent creatures that swooped and frolicked at her Lake of the Ozarks home each summer.

Once upon a time there was an unsuspecting gentleman who discovered the lady. One thing led to another and soon the gentleman married the lady and her hummingbird fetish. The collection began accumulating only "different" hummingbird items - hummingbird coasters and trays, hummingbird tiles and teasets, bowls and vases, nightlights and suncatchers - more little (and big) knickknacks than you can imagine.

Once upon a time the gentleman and the lady saw a hummingbird feeder made of glass and surrounded by copper. "Bill," said she, "you can do this."

And thus Ozarklake Distinct Decor was born. Well, the idea was born. The art is ever-developing.

We soon learned that patrons of the arts and crafts shows where we exhibit have a lot of questions about these wondrous little birds. A few years ago, Bill began working on a written compilation of answers to the questions he had been asked. This project grew and developed and you are holding in your hands the result of hours upon hours of research by both Bill and Terrie. We hope you find it interesting. Should you have suggestions for revisions, please let us know. This project, too, is ever-developing.

Contents

The *Family Trochilidae*

Distribution

The hummingbird is the *Family Trochilidae* consisting of 325 to 340 species in at least 102 genera, depending on how the classification system is interpreted. It is truly an American bird as it is found only in the western Hemisphere, from Alaska to Tierra del Fuego depending upon the season. The largest number of species, about 160, is found in Ecuador. Because a lot of their habitat has remained unexplored, new species are sometimes discovered.

About 21 species are seen in the US (the exact number sighted varies from year to year), but only a few are year-round residents in parts of western and southern states. Most species are migratory. The Rufous hummingbird may fly up to 3000 miles from winter homes in Central America to summer nesting areas as far north as Alaska. Even more amazing is the fact that hummingbirds do not migrate in flocks but travel alone. The young leave the nesting area last and fly to the winter home with no adult to guide them.

At least one kind of hummingbird spends the summer in just about every part of the continental US. Anna's are the only hummingbirds to typically spend winters in the US and Canada. The Ruby-throated, the species most commonly seen in the Midwest, is native to northern Central America and southern Mexico. The summer range of the Ruby-throated encompasses all of the eastern half of the United States and parts of Canada. The smallest species, about 2 ½ inches long, is the Bee hummingbird found in Cuba. The largest, appropriately named the Giant hummingbird, is about 8 ½ inches long and lives in the Andes.

 QUICK FACTS

Hummingbirds are most closely related to the insectivorous swifts.

Hummingbirds have no sense of smell but their eyesight is excellent.

Hummingbird legs are very short and nearly useless. They cannot walk in the common sense and most often will become airborne even to turn around on a perch.

Metabolism

A hummer's metabolism is astonishing. A hovering 3 to 4 gram bird uses about 35 calories per minute, breathing up to 250 times per minute. A hummer's heart is proportionately the largest in the animal kingdom and has a resting rate of 480 beats per minute and can reach up to 1260 beats per minute when excited.

The normal body temperature of the hummer is 103 degrees F but can be lowered below 60 degrees F in a state known as torpor. Torpor is not sleep but is a powered-down state used to control and conserve energy. People sometimes witness the torpor state as death and are astonished when the "dead" bird gets up, shakes itself, and flies away. In order to maintain this exceedingly high metabolism the hummer must feed at least every 15 to 20 minutes all day, eating twice their weight every day. Dawn and dusk see a higher feeding rate as the bird must quickly recover from a night of not feeding or get ready for the nightly fast. If unable to feed because of bad weather, a hummer may induce torpor and conserve energy until feeding can be done. In relation to relative body weight, hummingbirds require about 75 times as many calories per day as humans.

Hummer Diet

Hummingbirds have an utterly astonishing metabolism to support their frantic lifestyle. This energy comes generally from flower nectar and the sugar water in the feeders of hummingbird lovers. Protein is the primary food and comes from hunting small soft-bodied insects and spiders on visited foliage or on the fly by a behavior called "hawking". You can assist your hummers in the protein hunt by providing a small bowl of overripe fruit (banana peels are excellent) to draw the types of small insects hummers love.

 QUICK FACTS

Hummers are the smallest birds in the world but have the largest hearts pound for pound.

A hummer needs to eat about every 15 minutes all day. They consume about twice their weight daily.

A hummer's tongue is twice as long as its beak and has grooves on the sides to help it catch insects.

Note that for several weeks in mid-summer the hummers' use of nectar dwindles as they are concentrating on protein for the babies. During this time many people see fewer hummers and assume they are gone or that the feeder is not working. Don't lose hope or pull the feeders or let the nectar go bad in frustration; they will be back with the fledglings when they are ready.

Coloring and Feathers

The hummer's striking iridescent coloring has given them the nickname "Nature's Jewels". The color comes from two sources. The first is the pigment color of the feather and the second is a property known as structural color.

Interestingly, the pigment colors in hummer feathers do not include red or yellow. The feather pigment colors are limited to black, brown, and reddish brown. Structural color refers to the color reflected from the facets of the feathers and accounts for the shifting iridescence of the plumage. Hummer feathers may appear to be different colors when viewed from different angles.

White hummers, albino, are not unknown and are not a separate species. In the eastern US, an albino bird is most likely to be a Ruby-throated.

Sounds

The name hummingbird comes from the distinctive hum caused by the rapid wing beat in flight. Various species have distinctive hums as a result of beat rate and wing feather shape. Hummingbirds also have vocal chirps, chatters and buzzes to signal others, indicate mood, and to threaten. Most do not have a song as such though the Anna's hummingbird has been known to voice long "songs".

 QUICK FACTS

Hummingbirds are found only in the Western hemisphere and generally only in the tropical zones though several species migrate widely and range from Alaska to Tierra del Fuego.

Flight

In a world in which birds fly only forward, the hummingbird defies all logic and does it forward or backward, side to side, motionless in a hover, or even upside-down. This unique skill is because hummers get power on both the up- and down-stroke while other birds power on the down-stroke only and flap their wings at a much slower rate. In fact, in a hover, the hummer sweeps its wings in a flat figure-8 of about 50 strokes per second. This speed is above the human ability to focus and accounts for both the blur we see and the distinctive hum we hear. While performing his special courtship dance, a male hummer's wings may beat up to 200 times per second! Hummers have unusually large flight muscles, which make up about 25 percent of their total weight.

Life Span

Hummingbirds may live 5 to 10 years in the wild but it is not an easy life. Fledgling mortality has been observed from 17% to 59%, many lost to predation by hawks, crows, other large birds, and snakes. Accidents, high winds, cold, heat, or flood also take many young and adult birds every year. High winds are apparently a major factor in the migration of the Ruby-throated hummingbird across the Gulf of Mexico from the Southern US to Yucatan in Mexico.

Banding

The process of capturing and banding hummingbirds is used to study these largely unstudied birds. Capturing and banding may be done ONLY by researchers certified and licensed by the US Fish and Wildlife Service. There are currently about 80 authorized banders in the US and their work has significantly increased hummingbird data.

 QUICK FACTS

Hummingbirds can fly forward, backward, hover and even fly upside down. All except forward are very rare in other bird flight.

Hummingbirds are usually captured using a feeder placed in a drop-door cage or by the use of fine "mist" net corrals. Mist nets are illegal to possess except by licensed banders. After capture the birds are placed in special "holding blankets" usually made from the toe of a silk stocking. Each bird is banded with a tiny numbered band and its age, weight, bill length, tail length, and wing length are recorded. When all the data has been noted, the bird is offered a snack and then released.

Predators

Hummingbird nests are raided for eggs and chicks by snakes, large birds, and some mammals but adult hummingbirds are not regular prey. The most common danger is the family pet that gets lucky enough to ambush one. Birds, such as owls, hawks, roadrunners, and other large birds have been known to take hummers as have frogs, spiders, and preying mantises.

Spider webs also pose a hazard. Webs are very strong and sticky and the bird may become entangled and may actually be wrapped by the spider as just another large "insect".

Bees and wasps may attack a hummer and a single sting may be enough to kill the bird because of its small body.

There are reports of frogs capturing a hummingbird and one source reports a case of a hummingbird being taken by a BASS!

Though one would not consider plant burrs to be predators, there are three known cases of hummingbirds in Washington, DC, being fatally snared by burdock burrs in Rock Creek Park when they were not strong enough to pull the burrs from the plant.

Banding a Ruby-throated hummingbird.
Photo Credit: Ryan Haggerty, US Fish and Wildlife Digital Library Service.

QUICK FACTS

The Ruby-throated hummingbird, most common in the US, weighs about 1/10 of an ounce (just over 3 grams), about the weight of a dime.

A hummer's heart can beat 1250 beats per minute when active and as slow as 50 beats per minute at night.

The shiny feathers on a male hummingbird's throat are called a gorget.

About 21 species have ranges north of Mexico but only the Ruby-throated is usually found east of the Mississippi. Actually "east of the Mississippi" includes such states as Iowa and Missouri and east of the Mississippi is merely a rule-of-thumb. Of the species seen in the US, 16 breed here, 1 is a regular visitor, and 4 are seen rarely and are considered to be strays. Four species are regularly seen in Canada.

Hummingbirds are assigned to their own family under the Linnaeus system of classification – Trochilidae – from the Greek trochilos, small bird.

Normal body temperature is about 103 degrees F (40C) but it can drop to 70 degrees F (21C) at night.

Because of their small size and daring acrobatics, hummingbirds are rarely caught by predator birds.

Hummingbird bills can be categorized as either straight or curved downward (decurved). The curve of a particular species is related to the type of flower which is its most common food.

The fluid intake of a hummingbird is the equivalent of a 200-pound human male drinking between 400 and 800 pounds of water a day.

Males use their bright gorget as a signal flag to opponents and potential mates. Females generally have their most distinctive markings on their tails and will fan and wave the tail as a warning signal.

Rufous hummingbirds migrate from Central America as far as Alaska – a 12,000 mile round trip, longer than any migrating goose.

Hummers flap their wings from 20 to over 50 beats per second. This rapid rate accounts for the audible "hum" we associate with them.

Hummers' wing bones are fused into a stiff paddle, enabling them to hover.

Hummingbird Behavior

Mating and Reproduction

Hummingbirds court in the air but, contrary to common myth, mate on a perch. Males arrive first to establish a territory and food supply. They fly a courtship display when the females arrive, calling with a chirping sound and displaying his brightly colored gorget. Many species perform a flying dance to impress the female.

Once mated, the male takes no part in building the nest or raising the brood. The female lays a clutch of usually 2 eggs over a day or two, some as small as a coffee bean. The hatchlings are blind and have only a little down and a short bill.

A female may have more than one nest and may be building a new nest while still caring for an early brood. A third brood is not unheard of. Fewer females will be seen at the feeder while the hatchlings are in the nest as she feeds them insects she catches on plants or while flying (hawking).

The Rufous and Calliope hummingbirds have been observed to build a new nest on top of one from the year before. As many as four nests stacked up have been seen.

A hummingbird nest is about the size of a golf ball and about 1-inch deep. Spiderwebs are used to attach the nests to tree limbs.

Grooming

Hummingbirds care for their feathers using their bills and claws. They obtain oil from a gland near their tail and groom each feather. Head and neck are groomed by using their claws like a comb or by rubbing against a twig.

 QUICK FACTS

Hummers produce one brood per season and the males are not involved in raising the brood. A penny would cover 3 hummingbird eggs but there are usually only two in a brood. Eggs hatch in about 2 ½ weeks.

It takes about 3 weeks for the chicks to leave the nest.

Hummers sunbathe by facing the sun and fluffing their feathers out. They may also spread their neck and tail or spread one wing and then the other to catch the sun. Water baths are also a favorite of hummers and they will bathe in shallow pools, dipping their chins and bellies, splashing with their wings, or tossing water with their bills onto their backs. Hummers will also fly though a sprinkler, or fluff out in the rain to catch the water. They will perch and groom after bathing.

Traplining

Hummers feed by sight and will generally check out anything to see if it is a source of food. Our hummers seem determined that our wind chimes will someday be edible. Many birds follow a regular route through their territory checking out the food sources several times daily. This behavior is called *traplining*. Having a constant source of food on the route, either a hummingbird garden with successively flowering plants or reliable nectar sources, will go a long way in keeping hummers at your house all season.

Torpor

Torpor is a state in which a hummer's metabolic rate is only one-fifteenth that of normal sleep. Body temperature may drop by 20 to 50 degrees F and breathing may stop for a time. The bird's heart rate may drop from over 1000 beats per minute to as few as 50. Hummers go into torpor to conserve energy and in cooler temperatures as a survival mechanism. Often hummers which may appear to be dead are merely in torpor and will readily "recover" if disturbed.

 QUICK FACTS

Hummers like several baths a day and will fly in and out of sprinklers or splash in shallow pools and then sit and preen with bill and claws. Regular birdbaths are usually too deep for the tiny hummers.

A hummer may visit 1000 flowers in single day.

Thanks to excellent memories, hummingbirds often return to the same feeding area year after year.

Migration

Migrating species do so to breed. Hummingbirds are solitary travelers and the migration is separated by age and gender. Males begin moving north about three weeks before the females and depart the summer range before the females and juveniles. Some reasons are offered by experts for this behavior but the reason is more guesswork that solid fact.

One reason for the later departure north for the females is that a later trip will help insure that more food sources will be available. Hummers do not pair up and the loss of a few males will be less damaging to the species survival than the loss of females.

Conversely, the early departure of the males opens up the feeding area, usually highly protected by the males, for the new brood. The juveniles are the last to leave and migrate to the winter area without adult guides.

It is generally believed Ruby-throated hummingbirds fly non-stop across the Gulf of Mexico in the spring and possibly in both directions. This trip is believed to take a hummer 18 to 20 hours. This is a remarkable journey and certainly the trip carries the extra danger of adverse winds with little margin of error for the tiny travelers. Birds lose a quarter to half their body weight during migration. Scientists suspect the birds navigate by stars when traveling at night.

Anna's hummingbirds in the Pacific Northwest area of Washington, Oregon, and Vancouver do not migrate and may be stay nearly year-round at a feeder. Farther inland they do move as food sources dictate. Year-round birds are also found sometimes on the Gulf Coast and several species may winter in the Southwest.

An albino Ruby-throated hummingbird.
Photo credit: Missouri Department of Conservation.

QUICK FACTS

Baby hummingbirds cannot fly.

Changes in the climate and the numbers of hummer-friendly gardens in the US have helped to extend the range and duration of hummingbirds.

Hummingbird survival skills must be learned by the juveniles on their own, including flying, searching for food, avoiding predators, bathing, and grooming.

Thousands of New World plants rely on the hummer for pollination which occurs when pollen is transferred on their bills and head feathers from one plant to another.

White hummingbirds are rare in North America but some albino hummers are occasionally seen. Full albinos have white skin, bill, and feathers and red eyes.

Hummingbirds may live for 5 to 10 years. A female Broad-tailed was banded as an adult in 1976 and recaptured in 1987, at least 12 years old. A banded Ruby-throated was found to be 6 years 11 months and a Rufous was 8 years 1 month.

The Ruby-throated hummingbird was first identified by Carl Linnaeus, the originator of the modern classification system, in 1758 from a specimen from South Carolina.

The Hummingbird Clearwing moth is often mistaken for a hummingbird or baby hummingbird.

A female ruby-throated hummingbird.
Photo credit: John J. Mosesso/DBII.Gov.

Feeding Hummingbirds

Feeder History

Feeders were beginning to be developed about 1928 but a National Geographic article in 1947 used a newly developed strobe flash to show hummingbirds in flight at a feeder and interest was heightened outside the scientific community. In 1950 the Audubon Novelty Company offered an affordable feeder and hummingbird feeding has never looked back.

Today, feeders are offered in an infinite array of sizes and styles which are available nearly everywhere. What sizes and styles are best is a continuing argument among experts. While there are a few that have more desirable features, most properly placed and maintained feeders will provide food for the hummer and enjoyment for the feeder owner. Pros and cons of various readily-available feeders are discussed here.

Feeder Styles

There are nearly as many styles and types of hummingbird feeders as there are people who feed the feisty little birds. Hummers will regularly come to any feeder which is well cared for and well placed in an area where they have room to maneuver once they have located it. Other than these basic factors, one can start a vigorous argument about the merits and dangers of a particular style of feeder and which is best.

Almost all styles have advantages and disadvantages and there certainly enough styles to fit most any situation. Feeders come in plastic and glass; they come in platform, tube, and vacuum styles; and they hang, stick to the window, or stand in a hanging basket or window box. What follows are some general observations by myself and others about the various types.

Platform Feeders

Plastic platform feeders are available in nearly every discount, department, and hardware store in the country and range from very cheap to fairly pricey. This type usually has multiple ports in the top of a lower platform and may come with or without perches and bee guards. This feeder operates on the same principle as the vacuum feeder described below and uses a vacuum to hold the liquid in a container above the feeding ports. My early experience with the cheap feeder was that it very quickly deteriorated in the outdoors, cracked, had parts fall off, often developed annoying leaks, and required frequent replacement. Because these feeders operate on the same physics as the vacuum style feeder, they will leak if they have even the tiniest invisible crack or hole that allows air to enter them.

While it is interesting to see hummers perch on the feeder, there seems to be some disagreement about just how often that happens and even more about how often one will see more than one bird on the feeder. I have seen females and juveniles share a feeder late in the season but have seldom seen multiples feeding early in the season when the males are intent on chasing away interlopers at "their" feeder. I have one feeder hanging on a shepherd's crook and very often a hummer will perch there between sips at the feeder to stand guard. Hovering is not harmful and is the normal mode when feeding from a flower. While the ability to disassemble this feeder does make it somewhat easier to clean, it also makes it more prone to breakage and deterioration.

Vacuum Feeders

The vacuum style feeder is similar to a hamster watering bottle and operates by drawing a vacuum in the top of the feeder when it is inverted. There is a rubber stopper and feeding tube below the nectar container. The principal is similar to placing a finger over the end of a straw in a soda and lifting up some liquid. The most common complaint is that this style is prone to dripping. This can be true but there are several ways to reduce or eliminate the drips. The feeder should be nearly full before inverting, the stopper must fit air-tight, the *stopper should be wet* when inserted with a twisting motion, and the feeder should not be placed in direct sunlight all day.

Some of these feeders may be a bit harder to clean but it can be done if just a bit of time and care is taken. These do not have to be red or have red nectar and usually have a bright red tip on the tube at the nectar source. A new feeder or a feeder in a new location can be accented with a red bow or red ribbons to attract the birds. Once they have located the feeder, the red can be removed as it is no longer necessary. A translucent or transparent feeder does allow one to see the level of the nectar in the bottle but it does not take much monitoring to determine if the feeder needs filling, and it should be cleaned and refilled every 3 or 4 days anyway.

Female Ruby-throated at a vacuum feeder on the authors' porch.

These too can be simple or very ornate and run from inexpensive to works of decorator art. The primary problem with these is that there is a temptation to use a "standard" size stopper which is supposed to fit a soda or wine bottle. Unfortunately soda and wine bottles do not have a "standard" neck and if the stopper is even a bit loose, the feeder will leak and the owner will be very unhappy.

Tube Feeders

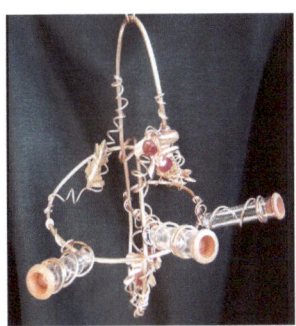

The tube style feeder consists of plastic or glass tubes with caps which have a hole in them. These are mounted in a hanger similar to a trumpet flower or other natural nectar source. These have the advantage of being easily replaced and easily cleaned but many consider their small volume to be a major drawback. A tube feeder with several stations seldom has all stations empty at the same time as the birds tend to sample each available tube in the same way they would a flowering bush. Part of the fun of the tube feeder is watching the birds flit from one tube to another. I keep several full tubes in the refrigerator and have them ready to change when I notice one empty and can clean and refill them at my convenience. A big advantage of this feeder is that it does not leak and seems to be more bee-proof. It is also very light and lends itself to being placed in a hanging planter or suction cupped to a window.

Nectar Cups

Another style has a shallow container which may be open or covered and may or may not have one or more hollow-stemmed artificial glass or plastic flowers stuck into it from the top. These also do not generally hold very much nectar and it is nearly impossible to keep pests out of an uncovered nectar cup. If hollow-stemmed flowers are incorporated, the bird hovers or perches on the cup and dips their beak into the flower to get  to the nectar. There are reports out there which say that hummingbirds have gotten their beaks caught in the feeder's flower. I have not personally seen this but I do not prefer this type anyway.

Location, Location, Location

Where to hang the feeder can be a difficult decision in which one has to balance the habits and likes of the bird with the natural desire to observe them. A new (first time) feeder is best hung near a flower garden, flower pot, or window box as that is one of the first places a hummer will check for food. Just as we recognize pizza, they know flowers. Once discovered as a food source, a feeder can be moved to a more viewable location in increments, taking care to maintain a feeder and hummer friendly environment.

Eventually a feeder can be placed very close to a window or a patio/deck and the hummers will continue to come. They are pretty fearless and learn quickly that the mere presence of humans is not a danger. Many have trained their hummers to hand feeding and this process, *for the extremely patient*, is outlined in *How to Get a Hummingbird to Sit on Your Finger.*

Some additional considerations are predators, sunlight, nearby cover, and animal pests. As fast as a hummer is, it is still vulnerable to predators. Probably the most common is the family cat. Though it would seem the cat could never catch a hummer, it does happen. Only the Calliope is known to regularly feed within 5' of the ground anyway. Keep this in mind when placing your feeder. Related is the animal pest, more a danger to the feeder than the bird but a real danger nonetheless, discussed in *Pest Control*.

Direct sunlight is the enemy of your nectar. Sugar water ferments very quickly as the temperature goes up and it goes up fast in an exposed feeder container. Nectar also molds. Fermentation is seen in the feeder as cloudiness; mold forms ugly black spots in the mixture or on the sides of the container. In either case, the birds quickly recognize an unpalatable, and possibly dangerous, mixture and will abandon that feeder for sweeter pastures and it often requires much time and effort to persuade them to return to that feeder when they have other food sources readily available. This is very likely the cause of the complaint that "the birds went away" or "they don't like the feeder". Note that there will be a lower level of feeding at the feeder during the time the female has chicks in the nest, a couple of weeks in late June or July.

Placing the feeder in shade and out of as much direct sunlight as possible will go a long way to keeping the feeder clean and active and reduce, but NOT eliminate, the cleaning and filling chore.

Temperature and sunlight are also contributors to a commonly-voiced dripping problem with vacuum feeders. It is simply physics that when a gas or liquid is heated, it expands and what is inside the feeder is a bit of each. When liquid expands it has to go someplace and that someplace is generally out the feeding tube in the form of annoying and unsightly drips. This probably cannot be entirely eliminated but keeping the feeder out of direct sunlight is one positive step.

Some recommend the placing of two or more feeders out of sight of each other to reduce the territorial squabbles that occur when a male takes "possession" of a feeder. This should have some effect, but we do like to have all the feeders in places they can be seen and dividing them makes this harder.

Introducing a Feeder

Because hummer feeders are a fairly recent development in the long history of the hummingbird, the birds do not instinctively recognize them as a reliable food source and must learn to recognize your feeder as such a source. This learning is aided by their natural curiosity and by watching the actions of other hummingbirds. When one bird begins to use a feeder, others are pretty quick to recognize that something good is going on there. This may help to explain the preference of one feeder over another of a different style; it's simply a matter of familiarity and the hummer may have decided to stick with a known thing. One way to assist the process when changing styles is to fill and hang the new feeder next to the old empty feeder until the hummer catches on to the new style. If we preferred a Whopper why would we look for a hamburger under a golden arch if we had never seen one; makes sense.

Red ribbons added to a new feeder. *Photo credit: Cam Schutte, KC, MO.*

Placing a feeder in a new location may be aided by hanging red ribbons or red bows in the area of the feeder early in the season. Red is the color hummers see the best and they will be sure to investigate the flash of color. It's comparable to the flashing "Eat Here" sign on diners! Once a feeder is discovered, the hummers commit its location to memory, so the red ribbons may safely be removed. Having a small mister or shallow birdbath nearby will also draw them to bathe, a regular activity for hummingbirds.

Window glass is one of the real dangers for hummingbirds in full flight. Feeders should be placed 15 feet from obstructions when hung. If you want your feeder closer to the window, it should be very close or even suction-cupped to the window so the bird is not tempted to fly around it and strike the glass.

It is quite normal for dominant male hummingbirds to chase other hummers from a feeder. Putting up a second feeder out of sight of the first feeder gives other hummers a chance to feed away from the bully.

Preparing and Caring for Nectar

Nectar for hummingbird feeders could not be easier to prepare. The recipe is:

One part ordinary white cane granulated sugar
Four parts water

Tap water is perfect. Distilled water is neither necessary nor recommended. It is not necessary to boil the water. A common myth is that boiling will reduce fermentation, but fermentation is not caused by anything in the water. Boiling will reduce the levels of chlorination and fluoridation in the water if you are using a system in which these are present. Boil the water, remove from heat, and stir in the sugar. Or simply mix the sugar into hot tap water. Allow to cool before filling the feeder. Sugar dissolves better in warm water, but even that is not required if care is taken to stir until all the sugar is dissolved. You can prepare more nectar than your feeder will hold. It will safely store in the refrigerator for up to 3 weeks.

This mixture is about the same sweetness as natural nectar (21%) and will not attract nearly as many insects as a more syrupy mixture (see *Pest Control*). There is actually some concern among some birders that the more sugary mixtures can cause liver damage in hummers. The 1:4 mix has been proven to be harmless and will provide the needed energy. Commercial hummer food is also not necessary and may actually be undesirable because of the added red coloring. They are also certainly more expensive and inconvenient than readily available home ingredients of water and sugar (sucrose).

There is no proven advantage of using one of the other sugars (glucose or fructose) and it appears that when given a choice, hummers prefer sucrose. If the hummers seem to be avoiding the feeder and your sugar does not specifically say it is sucrose, you can try changing to a brand that says it is pure cane sugar. DO NOT use raw sugar (difficult to get in the US due to pure food laws) as it contains a high level of iron which builds up in hummers and is fatal.

NEVER use honey, Jell-o, brown sugar, fruit, or red food coloring in your nectar mixture. Honey ferments VERY rapidly. Red dye is not necessary and some reports link red dye to tumors in the birds. Why take the chance?

The hummer feeder is really just a supplement which provides the hummer with the quick energy, the same energy as sugar fed to small children, to pursue the remainder of their diet – small insects.

Feeder Maintenance

Hanging a feeder confers a certain responsibility for healthy upkeep and one must be sure this responsibility can be honored when feeders are placed. Experts say hummers can detect fermented or moldy food and so there is a small, but real, chance of physical harm. The hummer will, however, quickly abandon a contaminated feeder in favor of good food and will have to be lured back, similar to a human avoiding a bad restaurant even after it has been reported to have become better.

Every week:

Note whether the nectar shows any cloudiness (fermentation) or mold (black spots) in the liquid or on the sides of the container. Fermentation means the feeder should be cleaned and refilled sooner; about 3 days at 80 degrees F and 2 days at 90 degrees F. Empty the feeder and flush with hot water. DO NOT use soap as hummers apparently do not like the residual taste. If mold is present, or just as a precaution, soak the feeder in a dilute bleach mixture of *¼ cup common bleach to 1 gallon of water* for an hour. The feeder should be rinsed thoroughly but any remaining bleach will be neutralized by the new nectar. Use a pipe cleaner to remove fungus from the feeding tube or nectar ports.

A bottle brush that reaches to the bottom and sides of the container is a great help. Another way to brush the inside is to put a small amount of uncooked rice or sand/small pebbles and some water in the feeder and thoroughly shake the feeder to dislodge the mold. Feeding tubes or feeder openings can be cleaned using a pipe cleaner. When the entire feeder is clean, rinse again and fill.

At least once a month:

Clean the feeder thoroughly with the dilute bleach solution described previously, brush and clean thoroughly, rinse and refill.

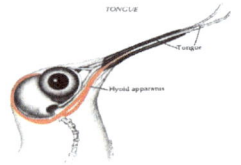

The tongue is divided into two equal lobes. It is attached to the hyoid appratus, which allows it to be extended well beyond the bill. This drawing is from "The Lives of Hummingbirds" (Tyrrell) and is posted at http://www.network54.com/Forum/439743/thread/1227456399/last-1227465276/Length+of+Hummingbird's+Tongue

There is an interesting lateral photo of a Ruby-throated Hummingbird skeleton, including the tongue, prepared by Stanlee Miller of Clemson University at http://www.hiltonpond.org/ThisWeek070115.html.

Pest Control

Four-Legged Critters

The most common complaints I hear are about the neighborhood squirrel population. Though not predators, squirrels are devastating to a feeder and will knock down and chew up whatever they can get their paws on. As bad, or worse, in our area are the raccoons that slip right up to the house at night. Anyone who has had seed feeders knows the continuing battle to defeat the squirrel. Tall slick poles, barriers, repellents, and B-B guns are all effective – sometimes and for a little while.

When you have a good feeder that you have paid good money for, the last thing you want to see is pieces on the ground. One tip is to hang the feeder from a closed eye using a snap gate D-ring such as is often used for keys. These are available in any hardware or discount store. Before I discovered the ring, I had added a "safety chain" along with the hanger to at least keep the feeder from hitting the ground. Why it took me years to think of the ring I have no idea. Your friendly squirrel or raccoon may still chew whatever he can get to and for that there is little to offer other than sheer inaccessibility.

Bees and Wasps

Bees, wasps, and yellow jackets love hummer nectar and can be a problem of safety for both the humans and the hummers. Bees and wasps are attracted to yellow and, sure enough, many of the flower decorations on commercial feeders are yellow. Getting rid of them or painting them red is a start. Many of the bee guard feeders also are the leakiest and the puddle outside the feeder totally negates the need for the guard.

The first action you can take when bees begin to take over is simply to move the feeder a few feet. Hummers are a lot smarter than bees and will quickly adapt while the bees may just assume the source is gone.

Another plan I have heard is to hang a second feeder with nectar of 3 parts water to 1 part sugar and reduce the hummer's feeder to 5 parts water to 1 part sugar. Separate the lower-sugar content feeder slightly from the old location. The bees will prefer the richer 3:1 nectar, the hummers will do fine on the 5:1 nectar, and the move should confuse the insects. If the feeder drips at all, it is necessary to keep the area of the drip washed down and clean.

Bats

While bats are not usually a problem in the Midwest, they can be in some parts of the country, particularly the Southwest. Some bats are also nectar feeders and pollinators and can drain a feeder overnight. A feeder with bee guards will keep them out or the feeder can be taken in at night. If taken in, you need to remember the hummers begin to feed just before sunrise and this is a critical feeding time for them.

Ants

Ants can be a real problem. In addition to being annoying, they can get into the nectar and die there. This is an unsightly mess and can contaminate the nectar. Ants can be deterred by the use of "ant guards" which hang between the hook and the feeder. Two kinds are generally available in birding stores and sometimes in the bird section of hardware stores. One is a cup which is filled with water and forms a moat the ants are not able to cross to get down to the feeder. The second type is an inverted cup between the hook and feeder which is smeared with cooking grease or commercial "tanglefoot" compound to deter the ants from crossing over to the feeder.

In the case of the moat, some recommend cooking oil in the moat but birds may see it as a water source and the oil is not a good choice. The oil may also get onto birds' feathers. In the case of the inverted cup, "tanglefoot" should be carefully placed so it cannot get onto the feathers of any bird which might come into contact with the ant guard. Hummers are so light that the "tanglefoot" might ensnare them.

One source recommends hanging your feeder from fishing line to discourage ants.

 QUICK FACTS

Hummingbirds are not generally found in grassland plains, which often lack sufficient nectar-bearing plants.

Hummers fly about 25 to 30 mph but can do 60 mph in a dive. The Violet-ear hummingbird can fly over 90 mph for short distances.

The smallest Hummer is the Bee hummingbird, in Cuba, about 2 ½ inches long. The largest is the Giant hummingbird at about 8 ½ inches long.

Other Feeder Guests

Many other birds and animals like the nectar and will often be seen trying to feed at a hummingbird feeder. Besides the obvious insects, lizards may find the nectar to be tasty. Orioles, chickadees, finches, and woodpeckers also like the nectar on occasion and will especially use feeders with perches although the lack of a perch does not always stop them from feeding. Some of these can be tempted away from the hummingbird feeder by placing a dish of fruit or fruit jelly out just for them or providing a nice suet block for the woodpeckers.

Frequently Asked Questions

When should my feeder be up and running?
The arrival and departure of hummers depends on the area and species. A state by state list is provided in *Hummers Are Found in 49 States*. In the Midwest we recommend having feeders out Tax Day (April 15) to Halloween (October 31) as a rule of thumb. Some hummers have been seen later and the feeders should come in earlier, at least temporarily, if there is an early freeze. Leaving the feeder up will not inhibit the bird's normal migration. They will go south when they sense it is time. The migration is related to hormonal changes and the decrease in daylight. A few occasional late stragglers may be seen as they migrate from northern areas.

I had lots of birds before and now I see very few!!
The number of birds you see in any year may vary a great deal due to a number of ecological factors. While some species are in decline or have numbers which fluctuate, the more likely reason is changes in weather which has altered the dependability of the local food supply. Extended heat, drought, or flooded areas at critical growing times may all affect the food supply, both nectar and insects. Conversely, a very good year for natural food may reduce the need or desire for hummers to actively use the feeder. These factors may combine or interact to affect the area in which they establish in any year and also affect subsequent years. A well planned and tended garden of hummingbird friendly flowers will also go a long way to attracting your own hummers.

I often hear the complaint, "I have had my feeders up for weeks and I had birds but now they don't come anymore!" This could be in the nesting period when the females are less active at the feeder or it may simply be that they are there but not at the moment you are looking - even looking away for an instant could miss one. However, I unfortunately believe many of these complaints are literally true and the feeder has been up for a month and has become totally unfit for hummer consumption. When a feeder is opaque and the nectar condition is out of view or a feeder is simply not carefully tended, the nectar goes bad and the hummers go elsewhere. In the heat of summer the limit really should be no more than 3 or 4 days, with the minimum in the hottest days of summer. It is just sugar water (if you resist the high-priced commercial preparations) and rinsing and bleaching is a small chore.

Another problem I hear often is that the feeder is hanging in a tree and the birds refuse to use it. One problem may be that a hummer's natural food is seldom in a tree and so they have no instinctive reason to see the feeder there as a food source. Another reason might be that while hummers nest in trees and perch in trees, the site is one they chose and in which they can be aware of surrounding danger. When head down and feeding, they are more vulnerable and skittish about being within a tree when other things are available in friendlier and more open places. This does not seem to be a hard and fast rule though as others report good results in a tree. Sometimes hummer preferences are a real mystery. Some feeders I have observed are 25 or 30 yards from a hedge row cover and the birds shuttle regularly back and forth to swarm the feeders. This distance is by necessity in the observed case and 15 to 20 feet is plenty.

There are, of course, natural dangers and predators about which we can do nothing. Nature is a tough place. I recently found on the internet a picture of a hummer which had been captured by a preying mantis. The family cat or dog is often the greatest danger and feeders should be placed well out of the reach of climbing or jumping pets. Unfortunately the best we can do is not make things worse.

 QUICK FACTS

A hummingbird will add up to one-half its weight in body fat in preparation for migration, a phase called hyperphagia.

How Does a Hummer Catch Bugs with That Long Bill?

A hummingbird catches flies at the base of its bill rather than at the tip. Most surprising, as the bird opens its beak to catch a fly, the lower bill suddenly bends downward at a point near the middle and widens, enlarging the bird's mouth to the detriment of the fly. The bone of the lower beak both twists and bends like a strip of thin plastic when the lower bill opens far enough.

You can get a feel for the remarkable bending action of the hummingbird's lower bill by cutting a narrow strip from the long dimension of a piece of typing paper, making a rectangle one inch by eleven inches long. Fold the strip in half along the short axis, leaving a **V** whose two legs are each one inch by five-and-a-half inches long. Hold an end between the thumb and forefinger of each hand, with the vertex of the **V** pointing away from you [see illustration]. Touch your thumb knuckles together while keeping your palms parallel to the ground. The paper "bill" should now be pointed straight out in front of you, ready to open wide. Rotate your palms together and you will see that the sides of the bill spread apart while the far end rotates downward, about an axis roughly midway

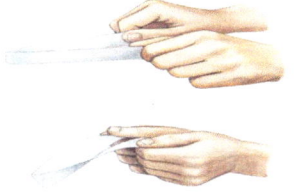

between your thumbs and the tip of the **V**. Like the narrow paper bill, the real hummingbird's lower bill splays apart into a shape that is far better-though certainly not ideal-for catching insects.

Illustrations credit: http://biomechanics.bio.uci.edu/_html/nh_biomech/ hummer/humm.htm

 QUICK FACTS

A hummer nest has an outside diameter of about 1 ½ inches and the inside is about the size of a penny. It is made of moss and lichens to be very well camouflaged and may be secured with spider web. The nest takes about a week to construct.

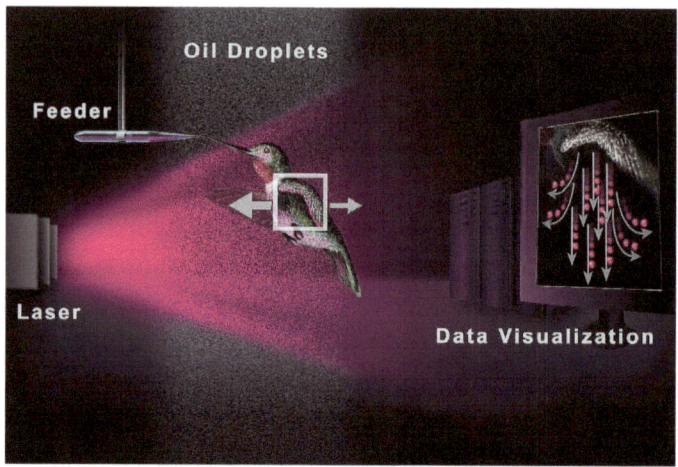

Researchers used digital particle imaging velocimetry (DPIV) to study the aerodynamics of hummingbird hovering. DPIV couples a digital camera that uses a laser light source and a computer to track circulating microscopic oil droplets seeded in the air. The system allows scientists to follow the movement of individual particles when air is circulated by the bird's wings. Credit: *Nicolle Rager Fuller, National Science Foundation.*

Researchers discovered that hummingbirds differ from both birds and insects in how they hover. Hummingbirds support 75 percent of their body weight on the downstroke, which is actually a forward motion in the nearly vertical hovering birds. The new finding will provide engineers with a refined model for developing miniature autonomous flying vehicles.

Credit: *Nicolle Rager Fuller, National Science Foundation.*

More information at: http://www.nsf.gov/news/
news_images.jsp?cntn_id=104268&org=IOS

What to Do "If"

If You Find an Injured Hummingbird

It is important to note that hummingbirds are wild animals and, as it is for all other animals, life is full of danger from weather, predators, disease or human intervention. The number of things humans can do to assist is limited and often not desirable no matter how much we would like to help.

Ruby-throated hummingbirds (*Archilochus colubris*) may fly into stationary objects and moving vehicles. Sometimes this kills them outright and sometimes it causes injuries that lead to the bird's death within a few days. Occasionally the hummer merely is stunned and can be rejuvenated.

Approach cautiously and get down close to the bird. Do the following close to the ground so that if you drop it, the bird does not have far to fall. Reach down toward the bird with both hands; sometimes this is enough to startle the bird into flight. If the bird doesn't move, gently cup both hands around it and lift it up and examine it more closely. If you see no sign of injury such as blood or a drooped wing or a broken bill, gently hold the bird loosely with the fingers pointed forward behind the head and insert its bill into the port in a hummingbird feeder. Gently slide the bill in and out of the feeder several times. If the bird decides to drink, its throat and crown feathers will move back and forth rapidly and the tongue may be seen moving in and out of the tip of the bill. Do not try to force it to drink.

If the bird drinks, the sugar water may be enough to stimulate it or bring it out of its stunned condition. If it does drink, place it in the palm of your hand and it may fly off.

It is against Federal, state, or provincial laws in the United States, Canada, and some other countries to keep a hummingbird in captivity without special permits.

QUICK FACTS

The tip of a hummer's tongue is fringed. The length of the tongue is rolled into two tubes and will extend past their bill to a distance about equal to the length of the bill.

Hummers have poor night vision and don't like to fly in the dark.

Hummingbirds have about 1,500 feathers.

If a Hummer Is Trapped Indoors

The first thing to do is to reduce the number of people and pets in the area to reduce the anxiety factor on the bird. The birds do not understand ceilings and their instinct to escape danger is to fly up.

If a hummer gets into your garage or house, leave the door open and hang a hummingbird feeder in the open door. The bird may find its way out. If not, a butterfly net can be used to carefully snag the bird so it can be gently released outside. You can also try holding a long-handled mop up toward the hummer; sometimes the bird will perch on the mop and you can lower it down.

One source recommends that you have a flashlight handy, close the door and turn on the garage light. When the bird is over a clear area, turn off the light and the bird should flutter to the floor as it has poor night vision and does not like to fly in the dark. Using the flashlight to locate it, gently scoop it up in cupped bare hands.

The bird's "exhaustion" clock is ticking and about 10 minutes will put it in danger. If nothing else is working, hanging a feeder high up inside may induce it to stop for a snack and extend the time to find a way to release it. Leaving the garage door open may be enough to get it out if it settles down and figures out the exit for itself.

If the bird is exhausted it may help to see if you can get it to feed as described previously under "injured".

Hummers in the garage are often the result of the red knob on the emergency release cord. The red knob is mandated to the manufacturer by the government but you do not have to keep it that way. It might be best to take the time to paint the knob some dark color - makes no difference to you and is better for the birds. At the very least, pull it up out of sight when the door is open.

If You Find A Baby Hummer

If a found hummer is feathered or has been seen to fly IT IS NOT A BABY. Hummers which are feathered and flying are fully grown juveniles and ready to leave the nest.

The best answer is "Leave baby birds alone." A young bird with feathers may be ready to leave the nest but may not be a strong flyer.

Typically the female will continue to feed the wayward fledgling as long as it is active and safe.

Hummingbirds apparently are unable to sense the baby has been handled so putting the chick back is an option (IF you can find the nest!) but unnecessary handling should always be avoided. If you do not find the nest, put the bird in a shrub or tree above ground and away from the family dog and cat. If a bird is not a true baby but is exhausted, it can be fed before being released using the method described under "injured".

Now comes the hard part. A naked or basically unfeathered bird is a true baby and unfortunately the best answer is for nature to take its course, as hard as this seems. All baby hummingbirds will not survive, and one that is out of the nest too soon may be defective in some way.

A mother bird may be away from the nest for what may seem to be extended periods as the fledglings get older. Mom (never Dad) may very well be nearby and watching or checking in periodically, or hunting bugs and on the way back. Chicks settled into the nest are probably OK and well fed but they will definitely be restless when they are hungry.

Hand-raising a baby hummingbird is very, very difficult even for professionals and is best left to those who know what they are doing AND keeping the bird is probably ILLEGAL.

If You Find A Dead Hummingbird

If you have a dead bird of any species, immediately wrap it in one layer of paper towel, being careful to keep the feathers as smooth and unruffled as possible. Put the wrapped bird in a zip-locking plastic bag, and then double-bag it. Put a tag in the bag with the time, date, and place where you found the bird. Place the bagged bird in your freezer and call your local college or university biology department or museum authorized to keep specimens. Good bird specimens are almost always welcome for research and teaching collections. If you can't find an authorized institution or individual to take the bird from you, you must dispose of it by burying it or giving it to your local animal control agency for incineration or burial. This is important in this era when Bird Flu is an ongoing, and hopefully not growing, problem.

If You Have a Hummingbird as Winter is Approaching

In the eastern US and in the area just west of the Mississippi River, the late season hummer is most likely not a Ruby-throated hummingbird but a wayward species which breeds in the West. The Rufous hummingbird which breeds in the far northwest and several varieties which normally occur in Mexico in winter have been seen in the US in fall and winter. Rufous hummingbirds seem to be able to adapt to cold as they can go into torpor and lower their body temperatures as much as 30 degrees.

Clean your feeder, make a fresh mixture of sugar water, and hang the feeder so the traveler can get fresh nectar. You probably will want to bring the feeder in at night and put it back in the morning if there is any danger of freezing temperatures to protect the feeder and to have unfrozen nectar for the traveler. In very cold weather it may even be desirable to have two feeders and to change them during the day to keep nectar available and palatable.

The Hummingbird Hawk-moth (Macroglossum stellatarum) is a species of hawk moth with a long proboscis, and is capable of hovering in place, making an audible humming noise. These two features make it look remarkably like a hummingbird when it feeds on flowers. *Photo taken by Yummifruitbat in September 2005 using an Olympus C-750UZ, licensed under the Creative Commons Attribution ShareAlike 2.5 License, at http://en.wikipedia.org/wiki/ File:Hummingbird_hawkmoth_a.jpg.*

 QUICK FACTS

Spanish explorers first found hummingbirds in South America and called them "joyas valadoporas" – flying jewels.

How to Get a Hummer to Sit On Your Finger

It is possible to get a hummingbird to sit on your finger or even to feed from your hand. There is a park outside Montego Bay in Jamaica where the Jamaican national bird, the Doctor Bird, has been conditioned to regularly come and sit on tourist fingers and feed from a tiny hand-held feeder bottle. It takes patience, a steady hand, and a good location, but hummingbirds appear to be pretty fearless and can be convinced you are no danger.

Place a good feeder at a comfortable height. Comfortable means a height you can hold a finger near for an extended period of time. Place a chair to allow you to hold a finger about 1 ½ inches away from the food location. Be sure pets or other people are not going to come near unexpectedly.

When a hummer has found the feeder and claimed it, you can go to the next step. This may take a couple of days but you will be able to tell that a hummer is guarding its food source.

When the feeder is in regular use, sit near the feeder within the reach distance you have determined, with your hands in your lap. The best time is probably in the morning when they are making up for the inactive night or in the evening when they are preparing for the night. You should be able to determine the peak time by prior observation. **DON"T MOVE! Remain rock still, even your eyes.**

At first the hummer will fly up and then zip away when he sees you nearby. If this is his normal feeder, he will not abandon it and will dart in to test the water and fly away. He may even hover very close by and check you out...do not move – freeze in whatever position he caught you until he is gone.

In short order he will decide you are not an immediate threat and take a quick sip from the feeder. Eventually he will get used to you being there and will feed normally, but if you move you will have to go back to the start until he is sure.

Repeat this over several days; wearing the same clothes so he will know it is you (hummers have very acute eyesight).

After acclimating him, hold your finger about a foot from the feeder to reinforce the change in position. Once again he will be hesitant but now should recover his confidence fairly easily since he knows it is you but somehow a bit different. Rock steady is still the key.

At intervals of feeding, move your finger about 2 inches and repeat until you are about 1 ½ inches from the feeder. The bird may initially feed while hovering over your finger but will eventually settle on it to perch.

Some birds do not like to perch while feeding or are more skittish than others, but patience will bring them around in most cases.

Another hummingbird person has gotten them to feed from nectar poured into the palm of their hand using much the same process but by eventually providing the hand of nectar and feeder together and then taking the feeder away leaving the hand as the only food choice. I have drawn them close (a foot or so) by a similar process using a tube feeder on the end of a short stick which I have acclimated in the area of a regular feeder.

The Jamaican National Bird
The "Doctor Bird" (Trochilus polytmus), or Swallowtail Hummingbird, lives only in Jamaica and is one of the most outstanding of all the species of hummingbirds. The feathers of the Doctor Bird are beautifully iridescent, a characteristic peculiar to this family.

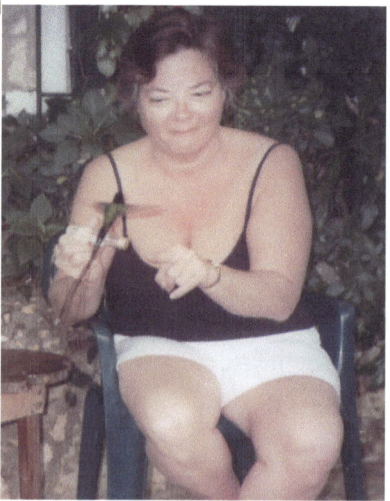

Terrie hand-feeding a Doctor Bird near Montego Bay.

Hummingbird Garden

A hummingbird garden provides natural food and an attraction to your feeders. It takes time and effort and a bit of a green thumb but is well worth the effort. An array of flowering plants which bloom all summer or bloom in sequence will provide for your hummers all season.

Hummers have no sense of smell so the flowers which attract them are those which have a high visibility and good nectar production. Hybrid varieties often make less nectar and so may be less effective than natural or heritage varieties. Your nursery should be able to help you choose plants which are suitable for your area.

There are many shrubs, flowers, and vines which produce great hummingbird flowers. Trees and shrubs can be chosen from those listed below depending on the space you have and the climate in your area.

Trees and shrubs which are hummingbird suitable are: Azalea, Butterfly Bush, Cape Honeysuckle, Flame Acanthus, Flowering Quince, Lantana, Manzanita, Mimosa, Red Buckeye, Tree Tobacco, Turk's Cap, and Weigela.

Some **vines** which produce hummer flowers are: Coral Honeysuckle, Cypress Vine, Morning Glory, Scarlet Runner Bean, and Trumpet Creeper.

Suitable **flowers** may be perennial or annual. Some perennials are: Bee Balm, Canna, Cardinal Flower, Columbine, Coral Bells, Four O'Clocks, Foxglove, Hosta, Hummingbird Mint, Little Cigar, Lupine, Penstemon, and Yucca. Annuals include: Beard Tongue, Firespike, Fuchsia, Impatiens, Jaconiana, Jewelweed, Petunia, several *Salvia* species, and Shrimp Plant.

Japanese Honeysuckle has been recommended but it is an exotic species which can quickly become invasive and should not be used.

Garden Supplements

It does not hurt to add feeders to the area near the garden flowers, box, or planter to supplement the nectar and to ensure it is available regardless of the status of the blooms. Tube feeders are good in this location as they fit right into the blooms. Other feeders should be about 4 feet up or so and should be protected from pets if possible.

Hummingbirds love to bathe but regular birdbaths are just a bit too deep for them. A very shallow dish with water will become the local hummer spa. Hummers also love to fly through a spray or mist and will zoom and loop through the water before perching to shake off and preen. A fine mister such as is used to mist plants will be much appreciated.

Pesticides

Using pesticides on your garden is NOT a good idea when you have hummers. First and foremost, the pesticides are a direct threat to the tiny and delicately balanced bodies of the hummer. Secondly, the pesticides kill the small insects and spiders which are the primary food of the hummer and provide the protein necessary to the hummer. If you would not eat it do not put it where the hummer can get to it, except for the bugs.

A trail of wake vortices generated by a hummingbird's flight. Discovered after training a bird to fly through a cloud of neutrally buoyant helium-filled soap bubbles and recording airflows in the wake with stereo photography. From http://en.wikipedia.org/ wiki/Hummingbird, illustration by Peter Halasz, licensed under the Creative Commons Attribution ShareAlike 2.5 License.

US Species Sketches

More than sixteen species of hummingbirds breed in North America. Eight are discussed here.

Ruby-throated Hummingbird (Archilochus Colubris)

Kingdom: Animalia
Phylum: Chordata
Class: Aves
Order: Trochiliformes
Family: Trochidae
Genera: Archilochus
Species: Columbris

Photo credit: Steve Maslowski
US Fish and Wildlife Digital Library Service.

This is the most common species in North America and is found in the entire area east of a north-south line from about the Dakotas to Texas.
Length: 3.5 inches (8.5cm)
Weight: 1/8 ounce (3.1 g)
Body Temperature:105 - 108 degrees F (40.5 - 42.2 C)
Breathing: 250 per minute
Heart rate: 250 beats per minute resting, 1200 beats per minute feeding
Wing Beats: 40 – 80 per second, average is about 52
Speed: Normally about 30 mph (48 kph), over 60 mph (over 100 kph) in a dive

The adult male has an emerald green back with an iridescent red gorget. The gorget feathers are not actually red and may appear to be black in some lighting situations. The male may sometimes display by raising the feathers around the gorget and shaking his head to show it off to the best advantage. The male is highly territorial and will fiercely guard his food sources, perching nearby and diving on any invader, pecking or bumping to drive them away from his territory. Even mating must occur on "neutral ground" and not in his territory. The male takes no part in nest building or care of the chicks and is smaller than the female.

The adult female is emerald green with a white throat and breast and a more rounded tail with white tips. Females will tolerate juveniles at the feeder for a time after fledging but eventually will also drive them away.

The sex of a juvenile is difficult to determine as they look a lot like an adult female. By August or September some males may begin to develop the gorget.

Anna's Hummingbird (Calypte Anna)

Kingdom: Animalia
Phylum: Chordata
Class: Aves
Order: Trochiliformes
Family: Trochidae
Genus: Calypte
Species: Anna

Photo credit: Stephen Tuttle, US Fish and Wildlife Service Digital Library System..

The Anna's hummingbird is the most common in southern California and is the largest. It is one of three, with Allen's and Costas, which are year-round residents.

Length: 3.5 inches (8.5cm)
Weight: 4.31 g (male), 4.07 g (female) – about 4 inches
Heart rate: about 1260 beats per minute resting
Wing Beats: 30 - 50 per second

It was named by the naturalist Rene Primevere Lesson for a 19th century Italian duchess Anna De Belle Massena, whose husband, Prince Victor Massena, had a specimen in his private collection.

The mating dance of the male Anna's hummingbird is an "air dance" or "pendulum dance". The male flies back and forth like a swinging pendulum and then dives down to make a loud pop at the bottom.

The Anna's hummingbird is the greatest consumer of insects of any North American hummingbird. It catches them on the wing in what is called "hawking". The normal habitat of the Anna's is chaparral, brushy oak woodlands, and gardens. Unlike other species, the Anna's has a song of sorts. The far northern range of the Anna's may be explained by their primary diet of insects.

The adult male is metallic green with a dark rose-red crown and gorget. His breast is grayish. The adult female has a green back, grayish breast, and a white throat with some red spots and white tips on some tail feathers. The juvenile looks like the female but may not have throat marks. Juvenile and female Anna's are often misrecognized as Ruby-throated hummingbirds outside their normal range. The Anna's is the only North American hummingbird with a red head.

Allen's Hummingbird (Selasphorus Sasin)

Kingdom: Animalia
Phylum: Chordata
Class: Aves
Order: Trochiliformes
Family: Trochidae
Genus: Selasphorus
Species: Sasin

Photo credit: Lee Karney, US Fish and Wildlife Service Digital Library System..

    The adult male Allen's has a metallic bronze-green head and back, iridescent coppery-red gorget (throat), rufous flanks. Males are smaller than the females. The adult female has rufous back and sides, white breast, white throat with some red spots, rounded tail with white outer tips. Young of both sexes look like the adult female. Allen's have been observed in Arizona, coastal California and Channel Islands, Georgia, Kansas, Louisiana, Massachusetts (Nantucket), Mississippi, Nevada, Oregon, Tennessee, Texas, Virginia, and Vancouver Island, B.C. Some birds migrate between Baja and coastal California, while others are year-round California residents.

Broad-tailed Hummingbird (Selasphorus platycercus)

Kingdom: Animalia
Phylum: Chordata
Class: Aves
Order: Trochiliformes
Family: Trochidae
Genus: Selasphorus
Species: Platycercus

Photo Credit: Marcus Martin, National Park Service.

    The Broad-tailed hummingbird is a medium-sized hummingbird with green upperparts and flanks, iridescent red throat, and gray underparts. Its tail may show some rufous. The adult female is larger with pale orange-brown underparts and lightly speckled throat. The Broad-tailed breeds in the mountains from eastern California and northern Wyoming through the Great Basin and Rocky Mountain states to southern Arizona and western Texas. They winter in Mexico. Preferred habitats include mountain meadows, pinyon-juniper woodlands, dry ponderosa pines, fir or mixed forests, and canyon vegetation.

Rufous Hummingbird (Selasphorus Rufus)

Kingdom: Animalia
Phylum: Chordata
Class: Aves
Order: Trochiliformes
Family: Trochidae
Genus: Selasphorus
Species: Rufus

Photo credit: Tom Smmiley, US Fish and Wildlife Service Digital Library System..

The Rufous hummingbird has been observed in every state except Hawaii and is the most widely distributed hummingbird in the US. It is one of the best fliers among hummingbirds and is able to dominate the airspace around feeders. It winters in Mexico and Panama and has one of the longest migration routes.

The Rufous has been described as "hateful" and the "junk yard dog" of hummers due to its extreme aggressiveness.

The female is larger than the male.

Rufous hummingbirds are very cold hardy and have been seen in temperatures down to nighttime temperatures of 0 to 20 degrees F.

The Rufous breeds as far north as southern Alaska, British Columbia and Alberta.

The adult male has a non-iridescent rufous crown, tail and sides. Its back may be rufous, green or some of each with an orange gorget and white breast. The adult female has a green back and crown with a white breast. The throat is streaked with rufous sides and base of tail feathers and white tips on the outer tail feathers.

Rufous means reddish color and the scientific name comes from the Latin for "rufous flame bearer". This is the only North American hummer to have rufous coloring on both the head and back.

Calliope Hummingbird (Stellula Calliope)

Kingdom: Animalia
Phylum: Chordata
Class: Aves
Order: Trochiliformes
Family: Trochidae
Genus: Stellula
Species: Calliope

Photo credit: US Fish and Wildlife Service Digital Library System..

The Calliope prefers a higher altitude and ranges in the mountain area from Texas to southern Canada.

The Calliope builds its nests over roads or streams and may repair a nest from a previous year or build a new one over the old.

Unlike many hummers, the Calliope feeds within 5 feet from the ground.

The bird was named for the Greek muse Calliope and the genus name means "little star". Ironically the name Calliope means "beautiful voice", which does not describe the birds call at all.

It is the only member of the stellula genus.

The Calliope is the smallest of the U.S. hummingbirds.

The bird has been described as a "fluffy ball of cotton with a toothpick sticking out of it". Both sexes have glossy green on the back and crown with white under parts and a relatively short bill and tail.

Adult males have wine-red streaks on the throat, green flanks and a dark tail. Its iridescent violet gorget has the feathers arranged in long rows. Adult females and juveniles have a pinkish wash on the flanks, dark streaks on the throat and a dark tail with white tips. Females are larger than males.

Costa's Hummingbird (Calypte costae)

Kingdom: Animalia
Phylum: Chordata
Class: Aves
Order: Trochiliformes
Family: Trochidae
Genus: Calypte
Species: Costae

Photo credit: John J. Mosesso/NBII.Gov

Costa's hummingbird is a desert species restricted to the far southwest and retreating just south of the border in winter months. Adult males have an extravagant loop and dive display that tells other birds its species and fitness. Its total distribution in both breeding and nonbreeding seasons is small. This, combined with widespread habitat destruction and alteration, has landed this bird on the Audubon Watch List.

Costa's have a light green back lacking rufous coloring on its short tail. Adult males have an iridescent purple crown and gorget (throat patch) that extends down around the outside of the chest (flared). Adult male Anna's have more red in their crown and gorget and their gorget is not flared. A female Costa's has gray underparts and may have a purple spot in the center of her throat. Females and juveniles are difficult to distinguish from Black-chinned and Anna's.

Adult males can be identified by their unique courtship display composed of three parts. The male first flies toward the object of the display (usually an adult female) and makes several passes over her. He then climbs steeply before making several vertical loops during which the male whistles. Loops can be 25-40 m high. The male finishes by zigzagging away from the female parallel to the ground. He shows up nearby soon afterwards and may repeat the sequence. He also whistles while perched, another way he can be identified in the field.

Black-chinned Hummingbird (Archilochus alexandri)

Kingdom: Animalia
Phylum: Chordata
Class: Aves
Order: Trochiliformes
Family: Trochidae
Genus: Archilochus
Species: Alexandri

Photo credit: Sally King/ National Park Service

The Black-chinned hummingbird measures about three and one-half inches long with a three and three-quarter-inch wing span. It weighs three to three and one-half grams, which is about equivalent to the weight of a dime plus a dollar bill. The male is dull metallic green above and gray below. He has a black chin and upper throat with a violet, iridescent gorget. A white upper breast looks like a collar against the gorget. The female lacks the characteristic coloring on the chin and upper and lower throat areas. From the side in poor light, it might be mistaken for a Ruby-throated.

This species typically pumps its tail more frequently when hovering than does the Ruby-throated Hummingbird.

Black-chins breed from southern British Columbia to Mexico. They winter in Mexico and arrive in Canada in late May. They begin returning to Mexico in late June. Most are gone from southern British Columbia by the end of July. They are abundant in southern Arizona throughout summer.

The Black-chinned is the western counterpart of the Ruby-throated. Their breeding ranges do not overlap, but the Black-chinned does occasionally wander into the eastern US in fall and winter.

"Archilochus" comes from the Greek "arch" which means chief and "lochus", a lady of people. Alexandri is named for the man credited with first identifying the species in 1846.

Hummingbird Species of the US and Mexico

Long-tailed Hermit, *Phaethornis superciliosis* —Mexico, Central & South America

Little Hermit, *Phaethornis longuemareus* —Mexico, Central & South America

Wedge-tailed Sabrewing, *Campylopterus curvipennis* —Mexico & Central America

Violet Sabrewing, *Campylopterus hemileucurus* —Mexico & Central America

White-necked Jacobin, *Florisuga mellivora* —Mexico, Central & South America

Green Violet-ear, *Colibri thalassinus* —Mexico, Central & South America

Green-breasted Mango, *Anthracothorax prevostii* —Mexico & Central America

Black-throated Mango, *Anthracothorax nigricollis*

Emerald-chinned Hummingbird, *Abeillia abeillei* —Mexico & Central America

Rufous-crested Coquette, *Lophornis delattrei* —Mexico, Central & South America

Black-crested Coquette, *Lophornis helenae* —Mexico & Central America

Fork-Tailed Emerald, including Golden-crowned, Colzumel's, and Canivet's subspecies, *Chlorostilbon canivetii* —Mexico, Central & South America

Cuban Emerald, *Chlorostilbon ricordii* —Cuba & Bahamas

Dusky Hummingbird, *Cynanthus sordidus* —Mexico

Broad-billed Hummingbird, *Cynanthus latirostris* -U.S. (Arizona, New Mexico, Texas) & Mexico

Crowned Woodnymph, *Thalurania ridgwayi* —Mexico, Central & South America

Xantus' Hummingbird, *Hylocharis xantusii* —Mexico

White-eared Hummingbird, *Hylocharis lucotis* —U.S. (Arizona), Mexico & Central America

Blue-throated Goldentail, *Hylocharis eliciae* —Mexico & Central America

White-bellied Emerald, *Amazilia candida* —Mexico & Central America

Azure-crowned Hummingbird, *Amazilia cyanocephala* —Mexico & Central America

Berylline Hummingbird, *Amazilia beryllina* —U.S. (Arizona), Mexico & Central America

Cinnamon Hummingbird, *Amazilia rutila* —Mexico & Central America

Buff-bellied Hummingbird, *Amazilia yucatanensis* —U.S. (Texas), Mexico & Central America (Belize only)

Rufous-tailed Hummingbird, *Amazilia tzacatl* —Mexico, Central & South America

Violet-crowned Hummingbird, *Amazilia violiceps* —U.S. (Arizona & New Mexico) & Mexico

Green-fronted Hummingbird, *Amazilia viridifrons* —Mexico

Stripe-tailed Hummingbird, *Eupherusa eximia* —Mexico & Central America

Blue-throated Hummingbird, *Lampornis clemenciae* —U.S. (Arizona, New Mexico, Texas) & Mexico

Amethyst-throated Hummingbird, *Lampornis amethystinus* —Mexico & Central America

Garnet-throated Hummingbird, *Lamprolaima rhami* —Mexico & Central America

Magnificent (Rivoli's) Hummingbird, *Eugenes fulgens* —U.S. (Arizona & New Mexico) & Mexico

Plain-capped Star-throat, *Heliomaster constantii* —Mexico & Central America

Long-billed Starthroat, *Heliomaster longirostris* —Mexico, Central & South America

Mexican Sheartail, *Tilmatura eliza* —Mexico

Sparkling-tailed Hummingbird, *Tilmatura dupontii* —Mexico & Central America

Lucifer Hummingbird, *Calothorax lucifer* —U.S. (Texas, Arizona, New Mexico) & Mexico

Beautiful Hummingbird, *Calothorax pulcher* —Mexico

Ruby-throated Hummingbird, *Archilochus colubris* —Eastern U.S. & southern Canada, winters in Mexico & Central America

Black-chinned Hummingbird, *Archilochus alexandri* —Western U.S. & Mexico

Anna's Hummingbird, *Calypte anna* (formerly *Archilochus anna*) — Western coastal U.S. & Mexico

Costa's Hummingbird, *Calypte costae* —Western coastal U.S. & Mexico

Bahama Woodstar, *Calliphlox evelynae* —Bahamas

Calliope Hummingbird, *Stellula calliope* —Western U.S. & Canada; Mexico

Bumblebee Hummingbird, *Selasphorus heliosa* —Mexico & Central America
Broad-tailed Hummingbird, *Selasphorus platycercus* —Western U.S., Mexico & Central America
Rufous Hummingbird, *Selasphorus rufus* —Western U.S. & Canada; Mexico
Allen's Hummingbird, *Selasphorus sasin* —Western coastal U.S. & Mexico

US Distribution by State

Summer months bring at least one species of hummingbird to every state in the US. except Hawaii, and warmer climates in the south may see some species year round.

Alabama – Ruby-throated hummingbird from mid-March to October.

Alaska – Rufous hummingbird from early May to October.

Arizona – (Note that many of these species are restricted to southeastern Arizona.) Broad-billed hummingbird from late March to September; White-eared hummingbird in summer; Cinnamon hummingbird (rare) in summer; Berylline hummingbird (rare) in summer; Violet-crowned hummingbird (rare) in summer; Blue-throated hummingbird from April to October; Magnificent hummingbird from late March to late October; Lucifer hummingbird (rare) from early April to October; Black-chinned hummingbird from March to October; Anna's hummingbird from January to June; Costa's hummingbird in spring; Calliope hummingbird from July to September and sometimes in April; Broad-tailed hummingbird from March to September; Rufous hummingbird from July to October and sometimes in winter and spring; Allen's hummingbird (rare) in July. Check with your local Audubon Society to find out which species are in your specific area.

Arkansas – Ruby-throated hummingbird from April to October.

California – Anna's hummingbird year-round. Other species seen throughout the state are Allen's hummingbird, Black-chinned hummingbird, Calliope hummingbird, Costa's hummingbird, and Rufous hummingbird. Check with your local Audubon Society to find out which species are in your specific area.

Colorado – Broad-tailed hummingbird, Rufous hummingbird, and black-chinned hummingbird from late April to September.

Connecticut – Ruby-throated hummingbird from early May to September.

Delaware – Ruby-throated hummingbird from early May to September.

Florida – Ruby-throated hummingbird from March to October. Vagrants from Central and South America are sometimes seen.

Georgia – Ruby-throated hummingbird from March to October.

Idaho – Black-chinned hummingbird, Broad-tailed hummingbird, Rufous hummingbird, and Calliope hummingbird from mid-May to September.

Illinois – Ruby-throated hummingbird from April to September.

Indiana – Ruby-throated hummingbird from April to September.

Iowa - Ruby-throated hummingbird from late April to September.

Kansas - Ruby-throated hummingbird from April to September.

Kentucky - Ruby-throated hummingbird from April to September.

Louisiana - Ruby-throated hummingbird from mid-March to October. Southern Louisiana may sometimes see western species that have lost their way.

Maine - Ruby-throated hummingbird from May to September.

Maryland - Ruby-throated hummingbird from April to September.

Massachusetts - Ruby-throated hummingbird from May to September.

Michigan - Ruby-throated hummingbird from May to September.

Minnesota - Ruby-throated hummingbird from May to September.

Mississippi - Ruby-throated hummingbird from March to October.

Missouri - Ruby-throated hummingbird from April to September.

Montana – Calliope hummingbird, Rufous hummingbird, Black-chinned hummingbird from mid-May to September.

Nebraska - Ruby-throated hummingbird from May to September (mostly in the eastern part of the state.)

Nevada - Broad-billed hummingbird, Magnificent hummingbird, Black-chinned hummingbird, Anna's hummingbird, Costa's hummingbird, Calliope hummingbird, Broad-tailed hummingbird, Rufous hummingbird, Allen's hummingbird from March to September. Check with your local Audubon Society to find out which species can be seen in your particular area.

New Hampshire - Ruby-throated hummingbird from May to September.

New Jersey - Ruby-throated hummingbird from April to September.

New Mexico – Blue-throated hummingbird, Magnificent hummingbird, Ruby-throated hummingbird, Black-chinned hummingbird, Anna's hummingbird, Costa's hummingbird, Calliope hummingbird, Broad-tailed hummingbird, Rufous hummingbird, Allen's hummingbird, Broad-billed hummingbird. Some vagrant species have been reported, such as White-eared hummingbird, Berylline hummingbird, Cinnamon hummingbird, and Violet-crowned hummingbird. Check with your local Audubon Society to find out which species can be seen in your particular area.

New York - Ruby-throated hummingbird from mid-April to October.

North Carolina - Ruby-throated hummingbird from April to October.

North Dakota - Ruby-throated hummingbird from June to August.

Ohio - Ruby-throated hummingbird from April to September.

Oklahoma – Ruby-throated hummingbird from April to October. Black-chinned hummingbird, Broad-tailed hummingbird, and Rufous hummingbird from October to December.

Oregon – Anna's hummingbird year-round; Rufous hummingbird, Calliope hummingbird, Black-chinned hummingbird from late February to September.

Pennsylvania - Ruby-throated hummingbird from April to October.

Rhode Island - Ruby-throated hummingbird from April to September.

South Carolina - Ruby-throated hummingbird from March to October.

South Dakota - Ruby-throated hummingbird from May to September.

Tennessee - Ruby-throated hummingbird from April to October.

Texas – Buff-bellied hummingbird; Blue-throated hummingbird; Magnificent hummingbird; Lucifer hummingbird; Ruby-throated hummingbird; Black-chinned hummingbird; Rufous hummingbird; Anna's hummingbird; Calliope hummingbird; Broad-tailed hummingbird; Violet-crowned hummingbird; Costa's hummingbird; Berylline hummingbird; Allen's hummingbird; Broad-billed hummingbird. Vagrants from Central and South America are sometimes seen. Check with your local Audubon Society to find out which species are in your specific area.

Utah – Broad-billed hummingbird, Magnificent hummingbird, Black-chinned hummingbird, Anna's hummingbird, Costa's hummingbird, Calliope hummingbird, Broad-tailed hummingbird, Rufous hummingbird from April to September.

Vermont – Ruby-throated hummingbird from April to September.

Virginia - Ruby-throated hummingbird from April to September.

Washington – Anna's hummingbird year-round; Rufous hummingbird, Calliope hummingbird, and Black-chinned hummingbird from March to August.

West Virginia - Ruby-throated hummingbird from April to September.

Wisconsin - Ruby-throated hummingbird from April to September.

Wyoming – Magnificent hummingbird, Ruby-throated hummingbird, Black-chinned hummingbird, Anna's hummingbird, Calliope hummingbird, Broad-tailed hummingbird, Rufous hummingbird from May to September.

In **Canada**, depending upon the location, four species are common: Rufous hummingbird, Ruby-throated hummingbird, Black-chinned hummingbird, and Calliope hummingbird.

If you see a solid white hummingbird, this is a very rare occurrence. First, get your camera! Then, call your local Audubon Society chapter immediately, as they will be very excited to have an albino hummingbird in their midst!

Summer Distribution Maps

Summer distribution maps are from the United States Geological Service, North American Breeding Bird Survey Results and Analysis, 1966-2003, .http://www.mbr-pwrc.usgs.gov/bbs/htm03/ra2003_blue_v2.html.

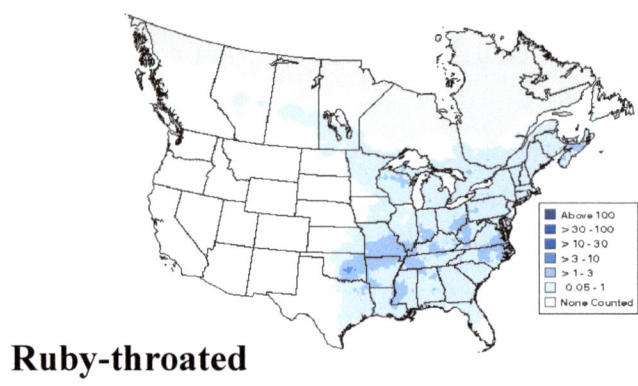

Ruby-throated

Black-chinned

Anna's

Costa's

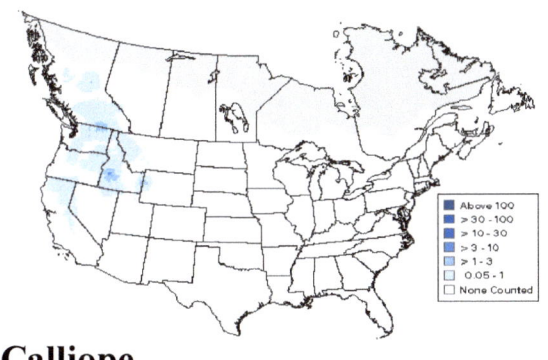

Calliope

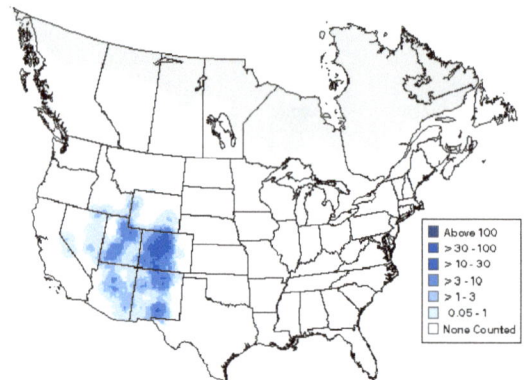

Broad-tail

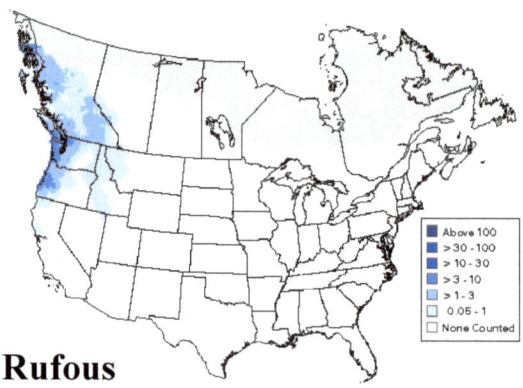

Rufous

Allen's

Myths and Misconceptions

Many myths and old-wives tales have evolved about the hummingbird. There are also some fairly strange facts that sound like myths. Here are a number of those myths, either confirmed or busted, and some interesting facts.

Hummingbirds migrate by riding on the backs of geese - BUSTED

Probably humans could not imagine this tiny bird flying the distances required at the frantic, energy-consuming pace they exhibit, but in fact hummers could give a goose a few lessons on migration. The Rufous hummingbird has been known to make a round trip of nearly 12,000 miles to Alaska. The adults are the first to leave the nesting area, with the new young following later without any adult guidance.

Hummingbirds cannot walk/have no feet – HALF CONFIRMED

In fact, a hummingbird's legs and feet are virtually useless for anything except perching. A hummer will usually fly up, even to turn around on a perch and will move only very short distances without flying.

Leaving feeders out past the usual departure time will cause hummers to stay and perish - BUSTED

The drive to migrate is stronger than any feeder and hummers will depart when nature and instinct say the time is right. In areas of the Southwest some species may be seen year-round, and there is some evidence that the Rufous species migration pattern is changing and some are wintering in the Southeast US. Surprisingly, the hummer is hardy and adaptable and may survive down to 20 degrees F. An article in the December 2003 *Southeast Missourian* described the confirmed sighting, and banding, of a Rufous hummingbird in southeast Missouri into mid-December.

A Hummingbird's bill is a hollow tube - BUSTED

A hummingbird has two mandibles; the upper half overlaps the lower. They can open the bill but there are limits as to how far it can be opened, about 3/8 of an inch. They can sometimes be seen flicking their tongue in and out – they do this to squeegee food from their tongue. Its tongue, which is forked at the tip, has a central trough. Dilute nectar sticks to the tongue tip and trough via capillarity action.

The hummingbird's tongue is hollow and they suck nectar like a straw - BUSTED

A hummer's tongue is not hollow. They lap up nectar like a cat laps water and squeeze if off the tongue into the mouth.

Hummingbirds hibernate in lake mud rather than migrating - BUSTED

No idea where this one might have come from. Only goatsuckers are known to hibernate. Hummingbirds in cold locales may go into "torpor" by lowering their body temperature and metabolism to conserve energy at night.

Hummingbirds only feed from red flowers - BUSTED

Hummers will feed from any flower they find to be rich in nectar.

Hummingbirds mate while flying - BUSTED

Hummers mate while perched. What may seem to be mating in the air is a part of the complicated mating ritual.

Birds become dependent on feeders and will starve if feeders are empty or removed – BUSTED

Because birds have wings, they instinctively forage for food, visiting many locations during the day searching for different sources. Birds never become dependent on one source and most studies have shown that birds with easy access to feeders use them for only 20% of their daily rations. If your feeders are empty or removed, the hummers will seek out other sources.

In the winter, the birds' feet will stick to metal perches – BUSTED

Birds do not have sweat glands, so their dry feet will not freeze to metal perches in the winter unless they have been wet by some other means.

Hummingbirds in Mythology and History

Hummingbirds in American Mythology

Hummingbirds are found only in the Western Hemisphere and are not mentioned in Old World literature until they were discovered here. Hummingbirds are found in many North and South American native legends and mythologies.

Mayan legend has the hummingbird as the sun in disguise courting the moon. Another Mayan legend says the first two hummingbirds were created from the leftovers after the creation of the other birds. The creator was pleased with the result and married the birds on a carpet of flowers in a ceremony attended by butterflies and spiders.

Mojave legend has early people living underground and hummingbirds being sent up to look for light. The bird found a path upward to the light where the people live now.

In the legend of the **Jatibonico Taino** people of Puerto Rico there is a story of a couple from rival tribes who were cast out but found a way to be together. One became a hummingbird and the other became a red flower. The hummingbird is believed to be a sacred pollinator with the mission of bringing life.

To the **Chayma** of Trinidad the hummingbirds are dead ancestors and may never be harmed.

The hummingbird brought tobacco to the **Arawacs** who called it the Doctor bird.

Both the **Cherokee** and the **Creek** tribes have stories of a woman who was courted by a Hummingbird and a Crane. The two agree to race around the world to see which will have the woman. In the Cherokee legend she believes the hummingbird will win but fails to realize the crane can fly all night while the hummer flies only in the day. In the Creek legend the crane flies straight but the hummer zigzags. In the end, the lady goes back on the agreement and takes the hummer because the crane is so ugly.

Hummingbirds often appear on **Hopi** and **Zuni** water jars as they were thought to have intervened with the gods to bring rain. Also in Hopi tradition, in a time of famine a boy made a toy hummingbird which his sister threw into the air where it came to life and began to bring them food. Eventually the bird went to the god of fertility and convinced him to restore the rains and allow food to grow.

Pima legend includes a great flood and the hummingbird takes the place of Moses's dove in bringing back news of dry land.

Baskets now used in Mexico in the Day of the Dead festival are said to have been originally woven by a **Taroscan** woman who was taught by a hummingbird.

Hummingbirds are used by **Pueblo** shamans as messengers to deliver gifts to the gods. For many Pueblo the hummingbird is the tobacco bird. The hummingbirds bring the smoke to the shamans to purify the earth. Also in Pueblo tales the hummingbird rescues the earth from a demon that catches the earth on fire. The bird gathers rain from the four corners of the earth and gains his bright colors when he flies through a rainbow.

Apache legend tells of a star-crossed couple who are separated but the man returns to her as a hummingbird dressed in the colorful war paint he wore when he was a man.

Early Spanish explorers were amazed by the elaborate cloaks made entirely of hummingbird feathers worn in **Aztec** ceremonies. Aztec chiefs wore hummingbird earrings. A mythical Aztec warrior was killed on the battlefield and a green-backed hummingbird rose up from the spot he fell to inspire the warriors on to victory. Every warrior who died in battle was believed to become a hummingbird after rising up to the sky and orbiting the sun for four years. Another legend has a hummingbird descending into the underworld to make love to a goddess who then gave birth to the first flower.

There is a folk belief in **Mexico** that the hummingbird can bring love and romance and stuffed hummingbirds were worn as charms for success in romance.

Hummingbirds in European History

Because there are no hummingbirds in Europe, the first explorers in the New World were awestruck with the beauty and diversity of the species and at first thought they were a cross between an insect and a bird.

Fantastic stories about hummers were popular. One said the bird stuck its bill into a tree in the fall and died only to be resurrected in the spring. A hummingbird skin was presented to the Pope as a gift soon after the birds were discovered.

Linnaeus, an early animal classifier, described 18 species in 1758 in *Systema Natura*. French naturalist Buffon cataloged hummingbirds and called them "flybirds"

An early writer about America, Hector St. John de Crevecouer was suitably impressed with the hummingbird and wrote this very accurate description of the hummingbird :

> *The humming-bird.*
> *It's bill is long and sharp as a coarse sewing-needle: like the bee, nature has taught it to find out in the calyx of flowers and blossoms those mellifluous particles that can serve it for sufficient food; and yet it seems to leave them untouched, undeprived of anything that our eyes can possibly distinguish. When it feeds it appears as if immovable, though continually on the wing... they are the most irascible of the feathered tribe. Where do passions find room in so diminutive a body: They often fight with the fury of lions... When fatigued, it has often perched within a few feet of me, and on such favorable of opportunities I have surveyed it with the most minute attention. Its little eyes appear like diamonds, reflecting light on every side; most elegantly finished in all parts, it is a miniature work of our great parent who seems to have formed it smallest and at the same time the most beautiful of the winged species*

The Story of the First Hummingbird

In 1902, the Houghton Mifflin Company published the *Book of Nature Myths* written by Florence Holbrook. Now in the public domain, this legend was found at http://www.sacred-texts.com/etc/bnm/bnm03.htm.

Part I. The Great Fire-Mountain

Long long ago, when the earth was very young, two hunters were traveling through the forest. They had been on the track of a deer for many days, and they were now far away from the village where they lived. The sun went down and night came on. It was dark and gloomy, but over in the western sky there came a bright light.

"It is the moon," said one.

"No," said the other. "We have watched many and many a night to see the great, round moon rise above the trees. That is not the moon. Is it the northern lights?"

"No, the northern lights are not like this, and it is not a comet. What can it be?"

It is no wonder that the hunters were afraid, for the flames flared red over the sky like a wigwam on fire. Thick, blue smoke floated above the flames and hid the shining stars.

"Do the flames and smoke come from the wigwam of the Great Spirit?" asked one.

"I fear that he is angry with his children, and that the flames are his fiery war-clubs," whispered the other. No sleep came to their eyes. All night long they watched and wondered, and waited in terror for the morning.

When morning came, the two hunters were still watching the sky. Little by little they saw that there was a high mountain in the west where the light had been, and above the mountain floated a dark blue smoke. "Come," said one, "we will go and see what it is."

They walked and walked till they came close to the mountain, and then they saw fire shining through the seams of the rocks. "It is a mountain of fire," one whispered. "Shall we go on?"

 QUICK FACTS

In the mid-1800's some species were made nearly extinct because of the demand for their iridescent feathers. Many of the species colorful names are in recognition of their striking appearance. Nine species remain at critical risk of extinction today.

"We will," said the other, and they went higher and higher up the mountain. At last they stood upon its highest point. "Now we know the secret," they cried. "Our people will be glad when they hear this."

Swiftly they went home through the forest to their own village. "We have found a wonder," they cried. "We have found the home of the Fire Spirit. We know where she keeps her flames to help the Great Spirit and his children. It is a mountain of fire. Blue smoke rises above it night and day, for its heart is a fiery sea, and on the sea the red flames leap and dance. Come with us to the wonderful mountain of fire."

The people of the village had been cold in the winter nights, and they cried, "O brothers, your words are good. We will move our lodges to the foot of the magic mountain. We can light our wigwam fires from its flames, and we shall not fear that we shall perish in the long, cold nights of winter."

So the Indians went to live at the foot of the fire-mountain, and when the cold nights came, they said, "We are not cold, for the Spirit of Fire is our good friend, and she keeps her people from perishing."

Part II. The Frolic of the Flames

For many and many a moon the people of the village lived at the foot of the great fire-mountain. On summer evenings, the children watched the light, and when a child asked, "Father, what makes it?" the father said, "That is the home of the Great Spirit of Fire, who is our good friend." Then all in the little village went to sleep and lay safely on their beds till the coming of the morning.

But one night when all the people in the village were asleep, the flames in the mountain had a great frolic. They danced upon the sea of fire as warriors dance the war-dance. They seized great rocks and threw them at the sky. The smoke above them hid the stars; the mountain throbbed and trembled. Higher and still higher sprang the dancing flames. At last, they leaped clear above the highest point of the mountain and started down it in a river of red fire. Then the gentle Spirit of Fire called, "Come back, my flames, come back again! The people in the village will not know that you are in a frolic, and they will be afraid."

The flames did not heed her words, and the river of fire ran on and on, straight down the mountain. The flowers in its pathway perished. It leaped upon great trees and bore them to the earth. It drove the birds from their nests, and they fluttered about in the thick smoke. It hunted the wild creatures of the forest from the thickets where they hid, and they fled before it in terror.

At last, one of the warriors in the village awoke. The thick smoke was in his nostrils. In his ears was the war-cry of the flames. He sprang to the door of his lodge and saw the fiery river leaping down the mountain. "My people, my people," he cried, "the flames are upon us!" With cries of fear the people in the village fled far away into the forest, and the flames feasted upon the homes they loved.

The two hunters went to look upon the mountain, and when they came back, they said sadly, "There are no flowers on the mountain. Not a bird-song did we hear. Not a living creature did we see. It is all dark and gloomy. We know the fire is there, for the blue smoke still floats up to the sky, but the mountain will never again be our friend."

Part III. The Bird of Flame

When the Great Spirit saw the, work of the flames, he was very angry. "The fires of this mountain must perish," he said. "No longer shall its red flames light the midnight sky."

The mountain trembled with fear at the angry words of the Great Spirit. "O father of all fire and light," cried the Fire Spirit, "I know that

 QUICK FACTS

In Navaho legend the humming-bird was sent up to see what was above the blue sky. It turned out there was nothing there. The hummingbird appears not only in Navaho myth but also in Mayan, Hopi, Zuni, Cherokee, Pima, Taroscan (Mexico), Apache, and Pueblo.

the flames have been cruel. They killed the beautiful flowers and drove your children from their homes, but for many, many moons they heeded my words and were good and gentle. They drove the frost and cold of winter from the wigwams of the village. The little children laughed to see their red light in the sky. The hearts of your people will be sad, if the flames must perish from the earth."

The Great Spirit listened to the words of the gentle Spirit of Fire, but he answered, "The fires must perish. They have been cruel to my people, and the little children will fear them now; but because the children once loved them, the beautiful colors of the flames shall still live to make glad the hearts of all who look upon them."

Then the Great Spirit struck the mountain with his magic war-club. The smoke above it faded away; its fires grew cold and dead. In its dark and gloomy heart only one little flame still trembled. It looked like a star. How beautiful it was!

The Great Spirit looked upon the little flame. He saw that it was beautiful and gentle, and he loved it. "The fires of the mountain must perish," he said, "but you, little, gentle flame, shall have wings and fly far away from the cruel fires, and all my children will love you as I do." Swiftly the little thing rose above the mountain and flew away in the sunshine. The light of the flames was still on its head; their marvelous colors were on its wings.

So from the mountain's heart of fire sprang the first humming-bird. It is the bird of flame, for it has all the beauty of the colors of the flame, but it is gentle, and every child in all the earth loves it and is glad to see it fluttering over the flowers.

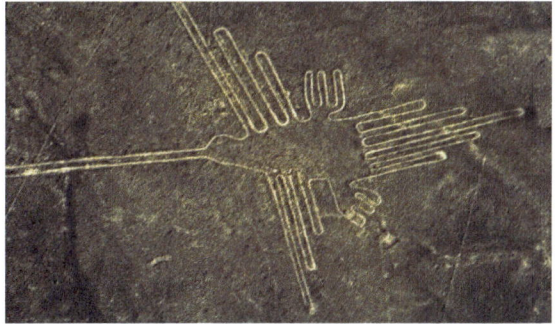

Aerial view of a giant hummingbird
geoglyph near Nazca, Peru.
Photo credit: © Philip Baird www.anthroarcheart.org

Native American Depictions

A Hopi Tocha (Hummingbird Kachina), date unknown, carved and painted cottonwood root, University of Michigan Museum of Anthropology, Ann Arbor, Michigan USA. A Kachina of the Kiva Dances of winter and Soyohim Dances in the spring.

"Totca, the Humming Bird, has a globular head painted blue, with long pointed beak. The dorsal part of the body is colored green, the ventral yellow. The rows of feathers down the arms are wings, by a movement of which the flight of a bird is imitated." *Fewkes, J.W. 1903. Hopi Katcinas (drawn by native artists). 21st Annual Report of the Bureau of American Ethnology, Smithsonian Institution, pp. 93-94.*

TOTCA

Glossary

SOURCE: http://www.mschloe.com/hummer/humgloss.htm

A

ACUTE: Having pointed tips, as in the tail feathers of many young birds.

AHY: After Hatch Year.

ALBINO: A mutant form in which pigments are lacking. A true albino hummingbird has pink eyes, feet, and beak and white feathers. A partial albino has some normal feathers and some white feathers.

ALBUMIN: The so-called "white" of the egg. See yolk.

ALPHA CODE: A system of abbreviations through which bird species are designated by four letters.

ALTRICIAL: Born or hatched naked, blind, and helpless. Hummingbird babies are altricial.

ANIMALIA: The Kingdom in which the Hummingbird is placed.

ANTS: Social insects (Formicidae) that often are attracted in such large numbers to hummingbird feeders that the birds stay away.

APODIFORMES: The Order that includes hummingbirds and swifts.

APODIDAE: The Family that includes hummingbirds.

ASY: After Second Year.

ASYMMETRICAL: Not symmetrical. Primary feathers in hummingbirds are curved and tapered and asymmetrical.

AVES: The Class in which all birds are placed.

AVIAN: Pertaining to birds.

B

BAND: A thin piece of metal, usually aluminum, that is formed into a ring that is placed around a bird's leg. The band is inscribed with a unique number that allows banders to collect information about sizes of bird populations, migration, longevity, and site fidelity.

BELLY: The part of the bird just ahead of the base of the legs.

BREAST: The region of a bird between the throat and the belly.

BREEDING RANGE: Area which breeding occurs.

BROOD: To protect nestlings by sitting on them; also, the whole complement of nestlings is a called a "brood."

BROOD PATCH: An area that develops on the belly and breast of birds—usually females—that are incubating eggs or brooding young. The area loses its feathers, becomes edematous, and shows increased vascularization—all of which helps the adult bird transmit its body head to eggs or chicks

BUTT BAND: A bird band for which the ends merely butt together when placed around the bird's leg. Birds such as hawks and owls require "lock-on" bands with end flanges that fold over each other to prevent the birds from removing them.

C

CALCIUM: An element essential to formation of eggshell and bone in birds. It is derived by hummingbirds through insects in their diet.

CALIPER: A device for making precise linear measurements. Used in to determine the length of the wing chord of hummingbirds.

CALORIE: A unit of heat, usually thought of as the amount of energy per mass of a substance. Gram for gram, fat contains more calories than carbohydrates, even though the energy in carbohydrates is often more quickly released by metabolic processes.

CARBOHYDRATE: An organic compound, consisting primarily of sugar or starch, that can be turned quickly into caloric energy. Hummingbirds get most of their carbohydrates from flower nectar or sugar water. Also see fat and protein.

CHICK: A nestling, i.e., baby hummingbird still in the nest.

CHORD, WING: See wing chord.

CHORDATA: The Phylum in which the Hummingbird is placed. It includes all animals that, in either embryonic or adult stages, have a notochord—a stiff rod that parallels the nerve chord. In vertebrates the notochord becomes the spinal column.

CLASS: The third highest main level of classification. The Hummingbird is in the Class called "Aves."

CLAVICLES; The "collarbones." In birds, the clavicles are fused at the tip to form a furcula, or "wishbone."

CLOACA: bird's single opening for solid and liquid wastes, as well as the reproductive cells (eggs or sperm).

CLOACAL PROTUBERANCE: A swelling of the cloaca in male birds, caused by the accumulation of sperm in a sac adjoining the cloaca; usually on visible in a bird captured for banding. In monomorphic species, the presence of a cloacal protuberance indicates the bird in hand is a male. The cloacal protuberance disappears during the non-breeding season when sperm are not being produced.

COEVOLUTION: The process by which, over time, organisms change in comparison to each other. The long, narrow bill of the hummingbird is a co-evolved adaptation that allows it to feed on plants with long, tubular flowers that, in turn, are adapted (co-evolved) for fertilization by the hummingbirds that take their nectar. See evolution.

CONGENER: A member of the same Genus.

CONTOUR FEATHER: See Feather, Contour.

COPULATION: Usually, the reproductive act by which sperm cells are transferred from a male to a female. In hummingbirds, the male has no intromittent structure (penis), so copulation consists of a quick touch of the tips of the cloacas of the two mates.

COURTSHIP: Activities performed prior to actual breeding. Hummingbirds, the male displays a noisy, aerobatic courtship flight that demonstrates his overall health to a prospective female.

COVERT: Feathers that cover the flight feathers (rectrices and remiges); e.g., primary coverts cover the bases of the primary wing feathers on a hummingbird and aid in streamlining.

CROP: A thin-walled food reservoir that lies between the throat and the gizzard of a bird. Food is stored there temporarily and the stored food can be regurgitated to feed young.

CROWN: The area on top of the head. It is sometimes appears yellow due to pollen deposits.

CULMEN: A standard measure used by bird banders; it is the straight-line measure of the top edge of the upper bill from its tip to the point where feathers begin to cover its base.

CUP: The depressed portion of a nest in which the eggs lie.

D

DIMORPHIC: Dissimilar in appearance. Adult males have colored gorgets and look different from females and young males that have white throats, so they are said to be "dimorphic." See monomorphic.

DISPERSAL: When an animal leaves an area and does not return. Different from migration, in which an animal leaves and returns, usually in a later season or year.

DOUBLE-BROOD: To attempt to lay a second set of eggs within a single breeding season, usually after a first brood has successfully fledged.

DOWN: Soft feathers that lie close to the skin surface of a bird and provide insulation.

E

ECOLOGY: The study of interrelationships among organisms and between those organisms and the environment.

ECOTONE: An "edge" where two distinctly different habitats blend together. Hummingbirds often nest in the edge between a wooded area and an open meadow or suburban yard; this ecotone usually contains plant representatives from the woods and the meadow, plus some distinctive species that may be found in edges but not in woods or meadow.

EDEMATOUS: Filled with fluid. When a brood patch develops in an incubating bird, the fluid connects beneath the belly skin of the adult female and enhances the transmission of her body heat to the eggs or chicks.

EGG: The female's reproductive cell, or ovum, after it has been fertilized.

ENDEMIC: Native to an area; see indigenous.

ETCHINGS: Tiny engraved marks on the upper bill of recently fledged hummingbirds. Just from the action of sliding the beak in and out of flowers, the etchings wear off over several months and can be used to determine the approximate age of the hummingbird.

EVOLUTION: The process of change over time by which a living thing changes from one distinct life form into another similar but different life form. See coevolution.

EYE RING: An area around the eye of a bird that is a different color from its surrounding feathers. An eye ring may be caused by the skin color of the eyelid, or by special feathers and may be "complete" (encircling the entire eye) or not.

EXOTIC: Not native or indigenous.

F

FAMILY: Fifth highest main level of classification.

FAT: A complex organic compound, usually ingested in the form of lipids, that is energy-rich but more slowly metabolized than carbohydrates. Tiny insects are the dietary source of fat for hummingbirds. Also see protein.

FEATHER: A specialized structure that covers the body and is found only in birds. Feathers may be modified for insulation, flight, courtship, and other functions.

FEATHER, CONTOUR: A feather that lies on the outside of the feather mass of a bird and defines its general shape. Contour feathers often aid in streamlining.

FEATHER, FLIGHT: A stiff feather in a bird's wing, usually the primary and secondary feathers.

FEATHER, PRIMARY: The long, asymmetrical wing feathers, attached to the ulna (forearm bone), that in hummingbirds are the main feathers used for forward propulsion.

FEATHER, SECONDARY: The shorter, more symmetrical feathers on the wing that lie between the primary feathers and the hummingbird's body. They are important in providing lift.

FEEDER: An artificial device, usually loaded with artificial nectar in the form of sugar water, that will attract hummingbirds.

FERTILE: If an ovum has been fertilized. Also, if a female is capable of producing ova.

FERTILIZE: To unite sperm and ovum, resulting in a zygote that typically develops into a new organism.

FIGURE-8: The path traced by the flapping wing of a Hummingbird that allows for— through changes in the shape of the wing's surface—forward, backward, and hovering flight.

FLANK: The side of a hummingbird, i.e., the area that lies underneath the wing when it is folded against the bird's body.

FLEDGE: To leave the nest, usually with the ability to fly or run.

FLEDGLING: A baby hummingbird that has just left the nest (fledged). Nestlings are usually fully-grown when the fledge and able to forage on their own.

FLIGHT FEATHER: See feather, flight.

FORAGE: To search for food.

FOREIGN RECAPTURE: See Recapture, Foreign.

FURCULA: The "wishbone." A structure unique to modern birds, formed by the apical fusion of the two collarbones (clavicles).

G

GAPE: The soft tissue at the corner of the mouth

GENUS (pl. GENERA): The sixth highest main level of classification.

GIZZARD: The muscular stomach of a bird. In hummingbirds, it is where tiny insects are ground up into digestible portions.

GONAD: A organ that produces reproductive cells. In male hummingbirds, the paired testes; in females, the functional left ovary.

GORGET: The throat feathers.

H

HABITAT: Where something lives.

HALLUX: A bird's hind toe.

HAREM: A social system in which a male hummingbird mates with several females. See polygamy and promiscuity.

HATCH YEAR (HY): A bird in the first calendar year of its life.

HAWK, SHARP-SHINNED: A small accipiter (Accipiter striatus) that preys upon other birds, including hummingbirds.

HOMEOTHERMIC: Able to produce one's own body heat (slang term is "warm-blooded").

HUMMINGBIRD: Any of 338 species of small birds in the Trochilidae. They are native only to the Western Hemisphere. Most are adapted for eating plant nectar, but all also take insects as a dietary protein source.

HUMMINGBIRD GARDEN: A garden filled with plants that produce nectar-bearing flowers attractive to hummingbirds. Gardens may contain native or exotic plants, or a combination of both.

HY: Hatch Year.

HYPERPHAGIA: Significant increase in feeding activity, probably stimulated by photoperiod, in which hummingbirds eat large quantities of nectar and insects and put on fat stores prior to migration; marked by an increase in mass of 50-75%.

I

INCUBATE: To sit on eggs, keeping them warm through the transfer of body heat, only the female incubates.

INCUBATION PATCH: See brood patch.

INDIGENOUS: Found naturally in an area. See native.

INFERTILE: Unfertilized by sperm. Hummingbird females sometimes lay infertile eggs that will not hatch. May also refer to a female unable to produce ova.

INSECTIVOROUS: To have the habit of eating insects.

IRIDESCENT: Displaying a shift in color hues. In male Hummingbirds, prismatic effects and scattering of light result in the gorget feathers appearing either black or brilliant metallic red, depending on the angle from which it is viewed.

IRIS: The pigmented portion of the eye.

J

JUVENILE: Pre-adult.

K

KEEL: The raised central portion of breastbone of a bird to which the large flight muscles (pectorals) are attached.

KINGDOM: The highest level of biological classification. Hummingbirds are in the kingdom called "Animalia."

L

LEUCISTIC: Appearing at first to be an albino because of white feathers, but having normally pigmented (dark) eyes, feet, and beak.

LIFT: A condition, caused by air flowing over a wing, that allows a bird to rise in the air.

LONGEVITY: How long something lives.

M

MASS: The correct term for an object's "weight."

MEMBRANE, NICTITATING: See nictitating membrane.

METABOLISM: The physiologic activity of an organism. Hummingbirds are said to have "high metabolisms" because their fast-paced activities burn energy at a rapid rate.

MIGRATION: When an animal departs an area and returns, usually in a later season or year. Different from dispersal, in which an animal leaves an area but does not return.

MIST NET: See net, mist.

MISTER: A device, usually hooked to a garden hose, by which a fine mist is sprayed to provide hummingbird with water for drinking and bathing.

MOLT: To lose feathers and then replace them. In Hummingbirds molting of the wing and tail feathers normally occurs on the wintering grounds. Some young (Hatch Year) males may begin to molt their white juvenile throat feathers in early fall before they migrate south; by the next spring those Second Year males that return will all have a complete set of colored throat feathers.

MONOMORPHIC: Having the same appearance (morphology). In most Hummingbird, adult females, young females, and young males all look alike and are said to be "monomorphic." See dimorphic.

MORPHOLOGY: External appearance.

MORTALITY: Death.

N

NATIVE: Found naturally in an area; indigenous. A native plant that is a natural nectar source for hummingbirds is adapted to the local habitat but may become choked out by invasive exotic plants from elsewhere.

NECTAR: A high-calorie, carbohydrate-rich, easily metabolized liquid produced by flowers. It is a major natural food for hummingbirds. (See also fat and protein.)

NEOTROPICAL: Pertaining to the New World tropics; i.e., the tropical regions of the continents and islands in the Western Hemisphere (including North, Central, and South America).

NEST: A structure in which the eggs are laid and chicks are raised.

NESTLING: A baby hummingbird still in the nest; also called a chick.

NET, MIST: A large (12m x 2m) device used to snare flying birds for banding. Birds are taken from the mist net quickly after capture and are banded and released unharmed.

NICTITATING MEMBRANE: The bird's "third eyelid;" a semi-transparent membrane that covers the eye while a bird is flying, protecting it from drying out.

O

OIL GLAND: See uropygial gland.

ORDER: The fourth highest main level of classification.

ORNITHOLOGY: The study of birds.

P

PECTORALS: The large paired flight muscles attached to the breastbone (keel) of a bird.

PENIS: The male intromittent organ that facilitates transfer of sperm. In hummingbirds, there is no penis, so copulation consists of the touching of the tips of the cloacas of the two mating birds.

PHENOLOGY: The study of change, especially with regard to changes that occur to due the seasons.

PHOTOPERIOD: The relative length of daylight to darkness. When days become increasingly short in autumn, it appears to stimulate hummingbirds to migrate south for the winter. Lengthening days in spring appear to be the cue to return to the breeding grounds.

PHYLUM: The second highest level of classification.

PIN FEATHER: A new feather, just being produced by the feather follicle, that has not yet flattened out and is shaped like a pin. See quill.

PLUMAGE: Feathers.

POLLEN: The male reproductive cell of a plant. Serves as one source of protein for hummingbirds that pick up pollen when they visit flowers to get nectar.

POLYGAMY: A social system in which a male mates with more than one female. Many hummingbirds are polygamous and are sometimes said to have a "harem." See promiscuity.

POPULATION: All the members of one species that live in the same area.

PRECOCIAL: Also see altricial.

PREDATOR: An animal that takes other animals as prey, usually killing them before eating them.

PREEN: To groom feathers with the beak or feet. Often involves anointing feathers with oil from the uropygial gland.

PREY: An animal that is taken by a predator.

PRIMARY: See feather, primary.

PROMISCUITY: Mating with more than one individual without forming a permanent bonds. Male Hummingbirds may be promiscuous because their relationship with a female essentially ceases after mating. See polygamy.

PROTEIN: A organic compound consisting of peptide-linked amino acids. Ingested by hummingbirds in the form of insects or plant pollen. Necessary to produce build and repair muscles, body organs, etc. Also see fat and carbohydrate.

Q

QUILL: A new feather just being produced by the feather follicle. When birds are undergoing molt and are partially covered by pin feathers, they are said to be "in quill."

R

RAPTOR: In birds, a hawk or owl that preys upon or scavenges other animals.

RECAPTURE, FOREIGN: A banded bird recaptured at a site away from where it was originally banded. Foreign recaptures provide information about dispersal, migration, and longevity.

RECOVERY: An encounter with a banded bird that is not alive, i.e., one that may have been killed when it flew into a window or vehicle, was taken but not eaten by a cat, etc. Recoveries provide information about bird dispersal, longevity and migration.

RECTRIX (pl. RECTRICES): Tail feather.

REGURGITATE: To bring food back up from the digestive tract after swallowing. Female hummingbirds regurgitate a slurry of nectar, pollen, and insects from their crops to feed their young.

REMIX (pl. REMIGES): Primary (wing) feather.

RETURN: An encounter with a banded bird that comes back to the same location where it was banded. Returns provide information about site fidelity and longevity.

RING: An international name for a bird band. Except in the United States, banders are usually called "ringers."

RIPARIAN: A habitat near water. Hummingbird nests are often found in riparian situations, i.e., near streams or ponds.

RUMP: The general area of a bird where the lower back and base of the tail join. The rump is sometimes marked with distinctive plumage. Hidden beneath the rump feathers is the uropygial gland.

S

SECONDARY: See feather, secondary.

SECOND YEAR: A bird in the year after the year it was hatched is a Second Year bird. The year begins on 1 January regardless of when the bird actually hatched.

SHELL GLAND: A gland within the oviduct of a bird that secretes calcium that hardens around the yolk and white to form an eggshell.

SHELTER: One of the important components of hummingbird habitat. Shelter includes places to hide from predators and the elements, as well as nesting spots.

SITE FIDELITY: The degree to which an animal returns to a specific site, usually at the end of its migrational route.

SPECIES (pl. SPECIES): The lowest major level of classification.

SUBPHYLUM: A sublevel of the Phylum level of classification.

SUGAR WATER: A standard mix of four parts water, one part table sugar that is placed in a hummingbird feeder as an artificial food source. The mix is high in carbohydrates but supplies no proteins or fats; hummingbird feeder mixes that contain minerals, vitamins, and proteins are commercially available but are relatively expensive compared to table sugar.

SUMMER: That period from June through August in which the majority of reproduction goes on. See winter.

SUMMER RANGE: The area of North America in which the Hummingbird breeds and spends the "summer" months (late March-September). See winter range.

SY: Second Year.

SYMMETRICAL: Showing similar shape; half of asymmetrical shape will be the mirror image of the other half.

T

TAXONOMY: The science of arranging organisms into groups, based on how closely they are related.

TERRITORY: An area, usually defended, in which an animal lives, feeds, and/or mates. A Hummingbird will defend a feeding territory that includes flowering plants and/or a hummingbird feeder.

THROAT: Also see gorget. The feathered "chin" area underneath the lower base of a hummingbird's beak.

TONGUE: The structure by which a hummingbird drinks nectar, using its brush-like tip to lap the fluid from flowers or artificial feeders. Hummingbird do NOT use their beaks like a straw to suck up nectar.

TORPOR: A overnight lowering of body temperature. On cold nights, a Hummingbird can lower its body temperature by about 15 degrees C (30 degrees F), thus conserving energy that would be required to maintain its normal temperature. The next morning, the hummingbird speeds up its metabolism and get its body temperature back up to normal (40.5 degrees C or 105 degrees F) within a few minutes.

TRAP, PULL-STRING: A device for capturing hummingbirds in which a feeder is hung within a trap. When a hummingbird enters the trap, the bander pulls a string to shut a trapdoor that captures the bird. The bird is removed, banded, and released unharmed.

TRIPLE-BEAM BALANCE: A device used for massing hummingbirds.

TROCHILIDAE: The Family name for all hummingbirds.

TRUNCATE: Having more or less squared tips, as in the tail feathers of many older birds. See acute.

U

UNDERTAIL: The region beneath the tail feathers, as in undertail coverts.

UROPYGIAL GLAND: A skin gland on the upper surface of a bird's tail that produces oil used to maintain feathers.

V

VAGRANT: A wanderer that shows up in unexpected places. Several species of hummingbirds native to the southwestern United States appear as vagrants in the eastern U.S., especially in late fall and early winter.

VASCULARIZED: To have increased capillaries and, therefore, increased blood flow. In a female bird with a brood patch, the belly skin becomes vascularized, and the increased blood flow more efficiently transmits her body heat to eggs or chicks.

VERTEBRATA: The Subphylum in which the Hummingbird is placed. A vertebrate is a chordate whose spinal nerve is protected by vertebrae of bone or cartilage (a "backbone").

W

WATER: An essential component of hummingbird habitat. In the wild, hummingbirds drink dew and rain drops and bathe in small pockets of water in leaves; they will also bathe by flying repeatedly through mist formed by a misting nozzle attached to a garden hose.

WHITE: The protein-rich layer that forms between the yolk and the shell of a fertilized bird egg. See albumin.

WING CHORD: A standard measure of bird wing length, from the bend of the bird's wrist to the tip of its longest primary feather.

WINTER: That period from October through mid-March when the birds are in Mexico or Central America. See summer.

WINTER RANGE: The region in which a Hummingbird spends the winter months (October through mid-March); this primarily includes Mexico and Central America. See summer range.

X

Y

YELLOW JACKETS: Wasps that sometimes monopolize hummingbird feeders in dry summer weather.

YOLK: The intracellular food reserve of a fertilized egg. In birds, the yolk is yellow and becomes surrounded by the white.

YUCATAN: A peninsula of southern Mexico that juts into the Gulf of Mexico. It is suspected to be the location where most trans-Gulf migrant Hummingbirds first make landfall.

Z

Green violet-ear hummingbird.
Photo credit: Ana Agreda/NBII.Gov.

*A variety of hummingbirds from Ernst Haeckel's
1904 Kunstformen der Natur (Artforms of Nature).*

Two hummers feeding at the author's home, August 2008.

The top two pictures are on my front porch, September 2008. The bottom picture was sent to me by Cam Schutte, a very happy customer of Ozarklake Distinct Decor.

www.ingramcontent.com/pod-product-compliance
Lightning Source LLC
Chambersburg PA
CBHW050809290526
45792CB00001B/43